On the Run

I Talk You Talk Press

Old Secrets – Modern Mysteries Book 3

Copyright © 2018 I Talk You Talk Press

ISBN: 978-4-909733-17-7

www.italkyoutalk.com

info@italkyoutalk.com

CONTENTS

ON THE RUN CHARACTER LIST

James Winchester has just retired, after being a diplomat for twenty years. Before that, he worked for the British Secret Service. He hopes to marry Sarah. However, his plans are upset by unexpected events.

Sarah Dumbarton is a retired schoolteacher. She lives in an old house in western Scotland. When she was young, she studied at university in Paris. She fell in love with another student, James Winchester, but he suddenly disappeared from her life, and Sarah returned to Scotland. Forty years later, she met James Winchester again.

You can read about James and Sarah's recent lives in books one and two of the Old Secrets - Modern Mysteries series: *The Blue Lace Curtain* and *End House*.

Archie Ross is the top policeman in Scotland. He grew up near the village where Sarah lives. He knows her well. When he was a young man, he worked for MI5. He got to know James well at that time.

Simon Birley met James when Simon was a code cracker in the British Secret Service. When he left the Service, he went to work at the British Council in Rome.

Other characters
Alberto has a business in Rome. He supplies fake identification to anyone who has enough money to pay for it.

Lorenzo Morelli is a bank clerk. He looks a little like James. This gives him the chance to make some money.

David Carver is the head of MI6. When he first joined MI6, James was his boss.

1. ON THE RUN

A tall, grey haired man crouched behind a row of garbage containers in an alleyway in the centre of Rome. On the ground next to him was a brick, and a gift bag from Babington's, the famous tea house near the Spanish Steps. He was looking at a group of workmen through a gap between the containers. They had finished work for the day, and were talking about going to a bar for a drink. The grey haired man waited and watched.

The workmen put their tools and overalls into their bags, and threw the bags into the van. The driver locked the van, and the workmen walked away. The man waited until they were out of sight. Then he ran to the van and hid behind it. He broke the back window of the van with the brick. He reached inside and took one of the workmen's bags. He ran back, picked up his carrier bag, and disappeared into a narrow gap between two buildings.

Ten minutes later, a man dressed in dirty overalls, and wearing a cap and heavy workman's boots appeared in the alleyway. He was carrying the heavy canvas bag. Inside the bag was a linen jacket, a pair of very expensive hand-made shoes, and the Babington's gift bag. He walked quickly towards the busy street and caught a bus. After about five minutes, he got off the bus and walked towards the river. He was in a working class neighbourhood. He turned into a narrow street that had several restaurants. He knew he had to get off the street. He went into a small family style trattoria. He needed time to think. It was dark inside. A few workmen were drinking near the bar, but the tables towards the back of the restaurant were empty. He ordered pasta in tomato sauce and a glass of wine.

When his order arrived, he drank the wine very quickly.

I am too old for this, he thought. *I'm retired. It's been almost twenty years since the last time people were chasing me. Who is chasing me? And why?*

He ate the pasta and ordered another glass of wine. He looked down at his hands.

I'm wearing workman's clothes, but my hands are not those of a workman. Workmen's hands are rough, but mine are smooth. They are the hands of an office worker. I'll have to find some other clothes and a room for tonight. The room will have to be somewhere a workman would stay.

James went to the counter and paid for the pasta and wine.

"I'm from out of town," he told the restaurant owner. "I've come to Rome to find work. I need a cheap place to stay. Can you suggest anywhere?"

"There are not many hotels in this area, but there's a small bed and breakfast in the next street. You could try there."

James thanked him, and left the restaurant. The room at the bed and breakfast was very small, but it was clean. He paid in cash for a room for one night. When he got to his room, he lay down on the bed and thought about what had happened. It had been a very strange day, and he was tired. Still, he couldn't go to sleep until he made some plans. He had to understand what was happening.

There must be a reason why someone is hunting me, he thought. *What was it? I must have missed something.*

He closed his eyes and let his mind run through the past week.

2. THE WEEK BEFORE

Today was Wednesday. Last Friday had been James' last day at work at the British Embassy. He had gone to farewell parties and lunches all week. On Saturday and Sunday, Rosita, James' housekeeper, helped him pack his belongings. The apartment and most of the furniture belonged to the Embassy, but James had many books and pictures. Everything was packed, and on Monday, a storage company came to take the boxes away. James had no plans for his retirement. He didn't even know where he wanted to live. He owned a house in Greece, but he wasn't sure he wanted to live there at the moment. Another idea was to rent an apartment in London. It was his hometown, but he had not lived there since he was eighteen. James couldn't decide, so he put everything he owned into storage.

Rosita left after the storage company took James' belongings away. She was retiring too. She was going back to her home village to live with her family. James spent Tuesday and Wednesday morning packing his suitcases, and making final arrangements to leave the apartment, and to leave Rome. By noon, everything was finished. He was booked to fly to London on Thursday to meet his friend Sarah. They planned to go to James' nephew's wedding together. Then James would spend a few days with her. He hoped that by the end of that time he would have a better idea of his future.

He went to have lunch with Simon Birley, an old friend from his Secret Service days. They were almost the same age, and had joined the Service at the same time. Simon was brilliant at maths, and was hired to work in the codes department. James was hired as a translator. His skill was languages. Their professional lives had turned out differently from what they had expected. James became a field agent, and Simon became a computer expert. James retired from the Secret Service when he was forty-five. After that, he joined the Diplomatic Corps, but Simon stayed on in the Secret Service until he was sixty. For the past few years he had been running the computer network at the British Council in Rome.

They had agreed to meet at a restaurant near Piazza del Popolo. It was one of James' favourite restaurants. James was a little late, and Simon was already sitting at their table waiting for him. He had a paper bag from Babington's Tea Rooms on the chair next to him. James smiled when he saw it. Simon was a tea drinker. He always bought his tea from Babington's.

They ordered, and settled down to enjoy their meal. Simon teased James about having no plans.

"You were always so organized when we were young. What's happened to you?"

James told him about Sarah, and that he hoped they would marry. He explained that it was hard to make plans until he knew if they would include Sarah or not.

"I wish you luck," said Simon. "I never met her, did I?"

"No. I've known her for more than forty years, but I never saw her during the time you and I worked together. You must be retiring soon. Are you still going to grow grapes?"

"I retire in three months. I've bought a house and small vineyard in Tuscany. The house is very nice, and the neighbours are friendly. I've been looking forward to it. But now I don't know how much time I'll be spending there."

"Why?"

"Oh. I have a few things to do first," said Simon. He didn't explain what he meant, and changed the subject. "Tell me, have you seen Archie Ross recently? He's Chief Constable of Scotland now. I find it hard to imagine Archie as a policeman."

"You know, I have! It was quite a surprise, but I met up with Archie in the summer. Sarah knows him too. We are going to stay with him after the wedding. But the three of us, Archie, you and I, should try to get together. Perhaps Archie and I could come and visit you at your vineyard."

They chatted about other old friends, and then it was time to go. James was due at the British Embassy at 2:30 to meet his replacement.

They walked to the cash desk. While James was paying, Simon was standing at the door looking across the street.

"I'm sure it will rain this afternoon. Of course I didn't bring an umbrella…" Simon stopped talking. He stepped back into the restaurant. He was holding the paper bag in front of his chest. James was putting the credit card receipt into his wallet.

"James. I've just remembered. I have a meeting at the Council. I'm going to be late. I'll have to go. But here," he handed the carrier bag to James. "A present to remember Rome! Give it to Sarah. Any woman would say yes to a marriage proposal over Babington's best tea!" He patted James on the arm, and he was gone.

James went to the Embassy. He was there for the rest of the afternoon. His replacement insisted on having a whisky to celebrate. It was 6:00pm before James finally left the Embassy. He almost forgot Simon's present. His former secretary ran out onto the street and handed it to him. "Come back and see us, please!" She smiled as she handed over the bag.

James decided to walk home. It would only take about half an hour, and he wanted to enjoy the streets of Rome. He didn't know when he would be back again. When he reached his apartment building, he stood on the opposite side of the street and looked up at his windows.

I am going to miss living here, he thought.

Then he saw a movement at one of the windows. There was someone in his apartment! He ran across the street and into the building. The elevator would make too much noise, so he went to the back of the lobby and climbed the stairs to the top floor. The building was tall and narrow, with one apartment on each floor. The door to his apartment was open. James crept to the door and entered. He could hear people speaking English. They were searching the living room.

"Nothing in the bedrooms, the dining room or the study," he heard a voice say. "He might have hidden something in the kitchen, or he's carrying it. We'll search the kitchen next. If there's nothing there, we'll get him when he comes back and find out if he's got anything. Have the others arrived yet?"

"Yes, they've just arrived," said another voice. "They're watching the front and back entrances. So there's no chance we'll lose him."

"What shall we do if he doesn't come back?" said a third voice.

"No problem. It's all been arranged with the police. They'll find him and hand him over to us."

James slipped into the kitchen. He took a kitchen knife from a drawer, and put it in the bag.

He opened the kitchen window, and climbed out onto a small balcony. The people watching the back entrance might see him, but he had to take the chance. The balcony was paved with stone tiles. James knelt down near the iron railings. He used the knife from the kitchen to remove one of the tiles. There was a small square hole under the tile. He took out two packets wrapped in plastic and dropped them into the bag.

He undid his belt and passed the handles of the bag through it. Then he fastened his belt again. He was going to climb, and he needed to have both hands free. He pressed himself against the wall of the building, and climbed onto the railing of the balcony where it joined the wall. He could just get his hands on the roof of the building. The building was made of rough stone, and he could find toeholds to help him. He pulled himself onto the flat roof. The buildings were very close together. The next building was one storey lower. James ran to the edge and jumped down onto the next roof. James jumped from one roof to another until he was in the next street. The last building was a small hotel with a rooftop bar. Luckily the evening was cold, and there was no one sitting at any of the tables. He opened the door and went down the stairs. He was in a hotel corridor. There was a fire exit at one end. He climbed down the fire escape to the narrow alley behind the hotel. He unhooked the bag from his belt, and looked for somewhere to hide. He saw a row of large garbage containers.

Perfect, he thought. *I'll hide there, while I think of some way of getting out of here.*

3. THE TV NEWS

Back in the bed and breakfast, James opened his eyes and rubbed them. It was no good. He could remember everything from the past week, but he still didn't know what had happened, or why. His arms and shoulders hurt. He was fit, but men of his age were not supposed to climb walls or jump across rooftops.

I'll go out for a drink, he thought.

He got off the bed, put his cap on, and looked in the tiny mirror on the wall. He looked like a workman, but his hands were a problem.

Most bars are dark, he thought. *So maybe no one will notice.*

He took some cash from his wallet and put it in his pocket. He put his wallet into the inside pocket of his overalls, and hid the workman's bag under the bed. He found a bar in the next street. It was crowded and dark. He bought a drink, and sat at a small table against the wall. The television above the bar was on the news channel.

A breaking news item came on to the TV. James got a shock. A picture of Simon Birley appeared. The newsreader said that Simon Birley, an employee of the British Council, had been walking across the Piazza del Popolo when he was hit by a van. A group of men had jumped out of the vehicle and grabbed him. They had thrown him into the back of the van, which then left the Piazza at high speed. Many people had seen the events in the Piazza, and taken photographs on their smartphones, and sent them to the TV station. Simon Birley's dead body was found by the river an hour later. A witness had seen the body being thrown out of a van.

"Police are looking for a Mr James Winchester, who ate lunch with Mr Birley just before he was attacked," said the newsreader. A picture of James then appeared on the screen. "If you see this man, please contact the police."

James pulled his cap down over his eyes. He left the bar, and hurried back to his room at the bed and breakfast. He locked the door and pulled the curtain across the window. Then he pulled the bag out from under the bed. He took out the paper bag that Simon had given him. It contained two packets of Babington's tea and a memory stick. James looked at the memory stick. He thought about when he and Simon were leaving the restaurant. Simon must have seen something, or someone on the street. He had put the memory stick in the bag and given it to James.

The memory stick must be important, thought James. *The men who took Simon and killed him must have been looking for it. When they didn't find it, they must have guessed Simon gave it to me. The men in my apartment must have been looking for it too. Who were they? They were not policemen, but they had connections to the police. Now the mystery men and the police are both looking for me. Why? What is on the memory stick?*

James shook his head. There was no point in asking these questions. He didn't have the answers. All he knew was that a group of people who spoke English had killed Simon and were looking for him. They wanted the memory stick. He remembered what the man in his apartment had said: 'We've arranged everything with the police. They'll find him and hand him over to us'.

Rome was not safe. The important thing was to escape, but how? Where could he go? He had many friends in the city. They could help him. But the police would be watching them. They might be listening to their telephone conversations. James smiled. He had other friends in Rome that nobody knew anything about. Friends from long ago. The police would not know about them either. James had been a very successful secret agent. One reason he had been so good, was that he knew people with very special skills. They were not particularly nice people, but they would help him, especially if he could pay them.

James sat down on the bed. He had credit cards, but he couldn't use them. The police would be able to find him. He had his mobile phone, but he couldn't use that either. But he did have the two packets he had taken from the balcony. The packets contained money - thirty thousand British pounds, and twenty thousand Euros.

It had been twenty years since James was a spy. He had often been in very dangerous situations. During that time, he developed the habit of hiding money for emergencies. Even after he became a diplomat, he still did it. You could never be sure when it might be needed. He often told himself it was no longer necessary, but it was a habit that had saved his life in the past.

James had enough money to keep moving, but first he had to get out of Rome, and then out of Italy. He thought very carefully. Finally he had a plan. It was not very good, but he couldn't think of anything else to do.

He looked at his telephone. Sarah would be traveling to London. She would arrive tomorrow. He had sent an email to say he would meet her at the railway station. He couldn't telephone her. If he spoke to Sarah, the police would know and they could trace him. Even worse, perhaps the mystery men who had killed Simon and searched James' apartment would find her.

He sighed. The news that the Italian police were looking for him would be on the English news by tomorrow. Sarah would know why he didn't meet her. He guessed he would miss his nephew's wedding too. It didn't seem likely he could solve this problem before Saturday.

4. ALBERTO

James waited until the streets were almost empty before he left the hotel. He was still wearing the workman's overalls and cap, and carrying the workman's bag. It was 2:00 am. The bars were closing. He found a taxi stand. When the first taxi driver heard the address, he refused to take him. "I don't go there. It's a very dangerous part of town."

James tried another taxi. He gave the driver the address. The taxi driver looked unhappy when he heard where James wanted to go. "That's a bad neighbourhood. The last time I was there, someone tried to rob me. I'll take you, but you have to pay me double fare. Are you sure you have enough money?"

"I got paid today," said James. "I have enough money."

The taxi driver opened the door and James got into the taxi. There was still a lot of traffic on the roads, but it was quiet compared to Rome in the daytime. The taxi driver drove quickly, and James relaxed a little. He hoped he could find Alberto's house. It had been a long time since he had been there. It was many years since he had seen Alberto, but he thought Alberto would remember him. The taxi stopped. "I'm not going any further," said the taxi driver. "These streets are not safe. You will have to walk from here."

James paid the taxi driver and climbed out of the taxi. Every big city has areas that are dangerous. James was going to walk through one of the worst areas in Rome.

A gun would be nice, thought James. *Pity I don't have one.*

He waited until the taxi drove away, then he walked quickly

through the dark streets towards Alberto's house. There was rubbish on the streets. Thin stray cats searched for food amongst the garbage. Very few of the streetlights were working, but James could see well enough to find his way. He walked fast, and after five minutes, came to a tall narrow building. All of the windows on the ground floor were covered with iron bars. James knocked on the door. He waited. There was no sound from inside the house. He knocked again. He stood back from the house, and looked up. A light came on in an upstairs window, and a curtain moved. James took the cap off his head so that the person could see his face.

He moved back to the door. A small slide in the door opened, and a face looked out. There was a long silence. "James?" said a voice. "Is it you, James?"

"Yes, old friend. It is James."

"Why have you come here? It isn't safe." Alberto sounded angry.

"I know. But I am in trouble, and I need your help."

"So you are in trouble. Why bring your trouble to me? Are you crazy?"

"Please, Alberto. The police and … other people… are chasing me. I must get out of Rome, out of Italy."

"So you are bringing the police to my door. I let you come in, and then in ten minutes or twenty minutes the police and these 'other people' will come here and arrest you and me."

"The police haven't followed me. No one followed me. I was very careful."

"OK. You were good at that. When we were young, you were the best. I hope you are still the best."

Alberto opened the door, and James hurried inside.

"Come upstairs," said Alberto. James followed Alberto upstairs and into a living room. Alberto closed the curtains and turned on the light.

"Sit, James. Let me look at you."

James sat on the old-fashioned sofa. Alberto pulled an armchair around, and sat facing James.

The two men looked at each other.

"Old age looks good on you, James," Alberto smiled. James thought that old age did not look so good on Alberto. He had lost most of his teeth. The few teeth remaining were brown and broken, except for one gold tooth. He was wearing old-fashioned blue striped pyjamas and a wool overcoat.

"You got me out of bed. I am an old man now. I am not in business anymore."

"Alberto. It is good to see you. I thought I was retired too. But it seems that trouble follows me. I don't know who is trying to find me. They seem to be professionals, and they can tell the police what to do."

Alberto looked past James to the corner of the room. James turned around to see what he was looking at. The room was old-fashioned, and not very clean. But in the corner was a very large modern television.

"You know, don't you?" said James. "You saw the news on the television. You heard my name, and saw my picture."

Alberto nodded. "Yes, I saw it. The men who took that Englishman from the Piazza del Popolo and then killed him, were very good. I don't think the police will ever catch them, or even find out who they are. Then I saw your face on the television. I could not believe it. Is Winchester your real name?"

"Yes it is. I have not been a spy for many, many years. I use my real name now."

"Maybe it was good I saw you on the television. I recognized you immediately, of course. I went to bed thinking about you. But I never thought you would come here. Why did you come?"

"I don't know who I can trust. I don't know who the police are watching. But I am sure that no one knows that we know each other. I only came because I need your help."

Alberto stood up. He went to a cabinet next to the television and poured two glasses of grappa. He came back and sat down, handing James one of the glasses.

"It's a strange time of day, and these are strange times. My friend James, who used to hunt people and trade secrets for the British, is now being hunted. But I wonder, old friend. Is it you that they want? Or is it something you have?"

James didn't answer. Alberto was very clever. He didn't know about the memory stick of course, but he had guessed that Simon Birley had given him something, or told him something.

Alberto reached out and patted James on the knee.

"Never mind. We have old secrets and new secrets. Maybe you don't trust me completely, but even so, I will help you."

14

James drank the grappa. At this time of the morning, it made him feel dizzy.

"Thank you, Alberto. Believe me, I trust you. But it is safer if you don't know."

Alberto smiled at him. "Maybe you won't thank me, James. I hope you have money. It will be very expensive."

James smiled back. "It was always very expensive. I remember."

"My services were very expensive because I was the best. I am still the best. I will find a perfect escape route for you. I have ways to get you out of Italy. But I think that will not be enough. Where do you want to go?"

"Maybe England," answered James.

"I think that's good. You say you don't know why you are being chased. Maybe that's true. But the man who was murdered was English. You are English. The answers will be in England. I am sure of this."

James nodded. He remembered that the men in his apartment spoke in English.

"Even if the answer is somewhere else, you have friends there. They can help you. So you must be able to travel in Europe, and from the European mainland to England. You know that the Italian police will talk to the police in other countries, and maybe the mystery men have many connections. So you will need a passport that everyone will believe is real."

"Even now? They say that the new electronic passports cannot be changed or copied."

Alberto laughed. "I am an expert. There are always ways. Trust me. Now I can see that you are tired. So you should sleep. I will wake you when everything is prepared. Just be sure you have enough money to pay."

Alberto took James to a small bedroom at the back of the house. He brought James some bottled water. When Alberto left the room, James took off the overalls and fell onto the bed. He was still wearing his shirt and trousers.

I shouldn't have drunk that grappa, he thought, as he fell asleep.

5. MAKEOVER

James stayed in Alberto's house all day Thursday. The time passed slowly. Sitting and waiting in the tiny bedroom, James finally had time to think about Simon. All the time James had known him, Simon was always so calm and relaxed. Simon had bought a vineyard for his retirement. Now he would never have the chance to enjoy it. What had Simon said while they eating lunch? He had 'a few things to do' before he could retire. What were these 'things'? The memory stick might give the answer. James and Simon had been very good friends for many years. James hated to think that he was gone.

I'll miss you, Simon. I hope whatever you were doing was worth it. You died for it. I will have to carry on. If you had a project, I should finish it for you, he thought.

He went to the bathroom and looked through the small cupboard under the basin. He found an old-fashioned razor, and took it back to the bedroom. He took the blade out of it.

He took off his belt. It was made from two layers of leather. He used the razor to undo the stitches on one side of the belt, near the buckle. He pulled the layers of leather apart and pushed the memory stick into the belt. It was not a good hiding place, but it was the best he could do.

In the morning, Alberto brought him bread and coffee. He came back at lunchtime with a bowl of pasta.

"It is more difficult than I expected," he said. "Your photograph is in all the newspapers, there are stories about you on English television, and all over the Internet. A normal fake passport will not work. I can do something else, but it will take more time. Give me your mobile phone. I need it. Also give me the clothes you were wearing when you met Signor Birley for lunch. I need your passport too."

James gave Alberto his mobile phone and passport. Then he got the jacket and shoes out of the workman's bag. He took off his trousers and put the overalls back on. He kept his belt. He was worried. *I am trapped here,* he thought.

"Don't worry." Alberto patted him on the arm. "I am the best. Just relax. But don't leave this room. There are other people in the house, and I don't want them to see you."

In the afternoon Alberto brought a young woman to the room. She was wearing high-heeled sandals, jeans, and a very tight T-shirt. Her hair was the colour of strawberries, and she wore large earrings. She was carrying a big bag.

"This is Alicia," he said. The young woman smiled at James. Then she turned to Alberto. "We'll use the bathroom. I'll need a chair. Can someone bring one for me?"

"I'll bring it," said Alberto. "I don't want anyone else to see him."

Alicia and James went to the bathroom. She asked James to sit with his back to the wall. She took a photograph from her bag, and taped it to the wall behind his head. "I usually take my grandfather's customers to my salon late at night, when everyone has gone home. It is more difficult to work here. But my grandfather says it is too dangerous to do that this time."

Alicia worked on James' face and hair for an hour. Then she pulled the photograph off the wall and handed it to James. Then she gave him a mirror.

"What do you think?"

James was amazed. Alicia had dyed his hair and eyebrows. He had a new hairstyle. She had changed the shape of his eyebrows as well. She had used a special glue to pull the sides of his mouth down, and also at the edges of his eyes to change their shape. She spent a long time making little plugs to put inside his nose to make it wider. He looked like a different person. He looked twenty years younger. But what was more important, he looked like the man in the photograph.

"You are amazing," he said to Alicia. "How did you learn to do this?"

"I went to beauty school. Then grandfather sent me to America to study makeup for the stage and movies. When I came back, he paid for my beauty salon."

James smiled at her. "I think you are very clever."

"Not so clever," she said. "This is good enough for entering another country on a boat or a train. But it is not good enough for airport security. You must stay away from places where the light is very bright, or where the security is very good. Of course you must wash and shave, so I have to teach you how to change the shape of your mouth and your eyes using this glue. Also, you must walk like a different man. The man in this photograph works in a bank, so maybe he is not very fit. Maybe he doesn't stand up straight. You can't just look like this man, you must be this man."

It was another hour before Alicia was satisfied. She packed up her bag and smiled at James. "I have another job to do for grandfather," she said. "Good luck." Then she left James alone.

He went back to the little room and sat on the bed. Finally Alberto came with more food and the bottle of grappa. He also brought a small suitcase, an airline carry-on bag, and clothes.

"I can get you to Dublin," he said. "After that you will have to do the best you can. I am sorry I can't get you to England, but Ireland is near enough, don't you think?"

James changed into the clothes. Alberto had brought everything – trousers, shirt, jacket, underwear, socks and shoes. He kept his own belt. Everything fitted perfectly.

"How did you get the size right?' he asked.

"I had your clothes. It was not so difficult to match the size," said Alberto.

"The suitcase has everything a bank clerk taking a short vacation to Ireland would pack," he said. "I have a car waiting to take you to near Milan. You'll change vehicles and drivers there. Then we have got you a ride to Ireland. You'll need your new identity when you get there.

"Your name is Lorenzo Morelli. It's lucky you speak Italian so well. It would have been difficult to find an identity for you from outside Italy."

He gave James a wallet. It was old and worn. Inside were credit cards, money, and a driver's licence.

"Is Lorenzo Morelli a real person?" asked James.

"Of course," answered Alberto. "He has given you his clothes, his wallet and his passport. He will disappear for a while. Later, of course, he will tell the police that his wallet and passport were stolen."

"Why would he do that for me?" asked James.

"Money, of course," said Alberto. "You would be surprised what some people will do for money."

"How did you find someone who is so close to my size, and who even looks like me?"

"Face identification software. We just searched the Drivers' Licence Database to find someone who looked like you. Lorenzo Morelli was the closest we could find in the time."

"How could you do that?" James was amazed.

"You have your secrets, I have mine," answered Alberto. "I have friends. And of course money helps. Morelli comes from the south. So I don't think you will meet anyone who knows him. Now you have to go."

James thanked Alberto and paid him. It took almost half of the cash James had taken from the balcony.

"I think you have something that other people want," Alberto said. "I hope you have hidden it well."

"I have something," James answered. "But I don't know what it is. So I don't know why it is so valuable."

"Valuable?" Alberto looked serious. "Dangerous, my old friend. Dangerous. Have a last glass of grappa with me. Who knows when we will meet again."

They drank together, and then went downstairs and out through the back door. A car was waiting.

"Take your bags in the car with you in case you have to get out quickly," said Alberto. They shook hands, and James climbed into the car.

The car sped through the streets of Rome and along the motorway on its way to Milan. At the same time, a man looking very much like James and wearing James' clothes was walking around the long distance trucks outside a highway café northwest of Rome. The man drank a cup of coffee in the café, then he walked back out to the truck park. He took James' mobile phone from his pocket, switched it on, and dropped it under the cover of a truck belonging to a French transport company. Hours later, a very surprised truck driver was stopped by police. They searched his truck looking for James, but found nothing, except the mobile phone.

6. LONDON

Sarah caught a train from Glasgow and arrived in London on Thursday afternoon. When she got off the train at Euston station she was surprised. She thought James would be there to meet her.

Perhaps he's been delayed, she thought. *Never mind, he told me he had booked rooms at the Royal on Thames. I'll go there.*

She took a taxi to the hotel. When she checked in, she asked, "Has Mr James Winchester arrived yet? I was expecting to meet him here."

The front desk clerk was young. He looked worried. "Just one moment please, Madam," he said.

He disappeared through a door behind the front desk. Sarah waited. An older man appeared through the door. "Mrs Dumbarton. I'm Anthony Barrows. I'm the hotel manager. We are delighted to welcome you here. I hope you will have a very pleasant stay."

"I am sure I will," answered Sarah. "I want to know if James Winchester has arrived yet."

"Uh, mmm…," the man seemed embarrassed. "We are not expecting Mr Winchester. I don't think he will be coming to stay here today."

"Really? Why not?" Sarah was surprised.

The man picked up a newspaper from a pile on the reception counter. He gave it to Sarah. "As you see, it seems that Mr Winchester is rather busy at the moment."

Sarah took the newspaper. On the front page there was a picture of James. The headline was 'Diplomat on the run?'

Sarah read the newspaper article. An Englishman named Simon

Birley had been kidnapped and murdered in Rome. He had been eating lunch with James just before it happened. Then James had disappeared. The police wanted to talk to him. They were looking for him. The newspaper said that the Italian police believed he had left Rome. They had asked the police in other countries to help them find him.

"Oh James! Where are you?" asked Sarah.

"I beg your pardon?" said Mr Barrows.

"Oh, I'm sorry," said Sarah. "I was talking to myself. This is a shock. I haven't seen TV or a newspaper since yesterday morning."

"I am sure it must be a real shock for you," said Mr Barrows kindly. "I see from our records that Mr Winchester reserved rooms for both of you. He is a good friend perhaps?"

"Oh, yes, yes. We were meeting here to go to a wedding. His nephew's…"

"I think you should come with me. I'll take you to your room," Mr Barrows said. He turned to the young man who was standing next to them. "Dennis. Please arrange for Mrs Dumbarton's luggage to be taken to her room. And remember, no gossip!"

Mr Barrows took Sarah to the elevators. As they rode up to the 4th floor, Mr Barrows chatted about the weather and the latest West End shows. "I went to see The Commitments," he said. "It was excellent. Of course I enjoyed the book, but sometimes the musicals based on books are disappointing, don't you think?"

Sarah wasn't listening to him. She was still trying to understand what had happened. The elevator stopped, and Mr Barrows led Sarah to her room.

"Actually, it's a small suite," he said. "It has a nice view of the river. I hope you will be comfortable."

When they were inside the room Mr Barrows said, "Mrs Dumbarton. I hope I can give you some advice. Please be very careful what you say to people. If the newspaper and television reporters hear that you were planning to meet Mr Winchester here, they will follow you everywhere. Your name and photograph will be in all the newspapers. I am sure they are already watching members of his family. And you say there will be a wedding. We don't want the young couple's day spoilt by reporters and publicity, do we?"

Sarah sat down in an armchair.

"Of course, yes. You're right. It is very good advice. I shouldn't have said anything downstairs. I was so surprised, I didn't think," she said.

"That is very natural," said Mr Barrows, smiling. "I suggest you relax. Shall I tell room service to bring you some tea or coffee?"

"No, thank you. I'm fine," answered Sarah.

"Well, I'll leave you then. Don't hesitate to call reception, housekeeping or room service if you need anything. Also, if the newspaper or television people bother you, please call me. I know how to deal with them."

"Thank you. You have been very kind."

"Not at all." Mr Barrows opened the door to leave, just as a porter arrived with Sarah's suitcases. The porter brought the bags into the room and left with Mr Barrows. Finally Sarah was alone. She realised she was still holding the newspaper. She read the article again.

Why did James disappear? she wondered. *Just because he had lunch with this man before he was kidnapped and killed, doesn't mean James had anything to do with it. Maybe James has been kidnapped too?*

The article in the newspaper seemed to say that the police thought James was connected to the crime. Sarah wondered why they thought that. She turned on the television and found a news report. The search for James was hot news, but there was no more information than in the newspaper. Sarah sighed. *Maybe James will contact me.*

Sarah took a shower and changed. She took her dress for the wedding out of her suitcase, and hung it in the closet.

I wonder if I'll be wearing that? I hope so. It's a beautiful dress, and I think I look good in it.

Sarah sat in the living room of the suite and tried to watch television. It was no good. She couldn't concentrate. She wondered if she should call James' sister. The problem was that she knew Andy, James' nephew, who was getting married on Saturday. But she had never met anyone else from James' family.

It was all very difficult. Sarah realized she was hungry. She called room service and ordered an omelette. When there was a knock on her door about thirty minutes later, she went and looked through the spy hole in the door. It was a waiter with a food cart. She opened the door and let him in. The waiter arranged everything for her meal on the table in the living area and left. Sarah sat down to eat. She lifted the cover on the plate. The omelette looked delicious. Then she saw a piece of paper under the plate. Sarah read the note on it, and suddenly she wasn't hungry any more.

---*Sarah. I think you would like to take a walk. Look out the window. I will be on the other side of the river in 15 minutes time. It is very important that we talk. A---*

Sarah ran to the window and looked out. A man was standing on the other side of the road, talking on a mobile phone. It was getting dark, so the streetlights were on. As she looked out, the man glanced up. He moved and stood under a streetlight. She could see his face. It was Archie Ross! Sarah waved, but he had gone. She put on her jacket, and grabbed her bag and room key. She ran to the elevator. It took her about five minutes to cross Waterloo Bridge. As she passed a bus stop at other end of the bridge, a car stopped next to her. The back door opened, and she could see Archie in the back seat.

"Get in," said Archie.

Sarah climbed into the car. She shut the door, and the car moved off. Archie reached out and hugged her.

"Oh Archie," said Sarah "What is happening? Do the police think James has been kidnapped?"

"No, Sarah," said Archie. "They think that he is the leader of the men who kidnapped and murdered Simon Birley."

"That's ridiculous. James couldn't kill anyone!" Sarah was angry.

Archie held Sarah's hands. "No, Sarah. It is not ridiculous. These days James is the perfect gentleman. The retired diplomat. But you know about his past. You know what he did for more than twenty years. Of course he could kill someone! But one thing I am sure about. James didn't kill Simon Birley. That's impossible. Simon was one of James' closest friends."

"It was very kind of you to come to talk to me, Archie," said Sarah.

"I didn't come to talk to you, Sarah. I work in Scotland, but everyone knows James and I are friends. The English police asked me to come here to help them. I agreed to come because I thought I could help James.

"I think that maybe he will find a way to contact you. If he does, you must give him a message. You must tell him that this is not just the police. I don't know why, but the secret services of every country in Europe, and even the USA are looking for him. People are talking about terrorists, chemical weapons, and even the possibility of nuclear weapons. The police are the least of his problems. I'm trying to find out what has happened, but James has no friends now. If he contacts you, you must tell him to trust nobody."

Sarah said nothing. She looked out the window.

"Where are we?"

"We have driven back across the river. We're almost back at the hotel. We will stop alongside the river so you can walk back."

"Archie?"

"Yes, Sarah?"

"Why didn't you come to my hotel room to tell me this?"

"Sarah! I don't think you understand how serious this is. Your room may be bugged. I'm sure someone will listen to every phone call you make. The newspapers and television haven't found out about your friendship with James yet, but the police and secret service know. Try to behave normally. Go to the wedding. Have a nice time. But don't talk to anybody about James, and don't trust anyone. Tony Barrows, the hotel manager, is OK. He's an old friend. He called me after you arrived. I asked him to give you the note. If you have any trouble, tell Tony. He will find a way to contact me. And be careful!"

7. TRACEY

Fifty kilometres from London, in a house near Tonbridge, Tracey Bixton was waiting to try on her wedding dress. She was feeling pleased. On Saturday, she would marry Andy Fairweather. She expected her life would be very comfortable after that. She looked around her bedroom in Andy's parents' house. It was large and old-fashioned. The curtains, bed cover and walls were all covered in the same pattern. It was white, with a pattern of blue flowers and peacocks. All the furniture seemed to be antique. It was not Tracey's style, but she liked the idea that it must all be very expensive.

I've been very smart, she thought. *No more money worries for me!*

She walked over to the long mirror on the wall and looked at herself. Tracey's hair was long and blonde. Her eyes were pale blue. She wore a lot of make-up and very short skirts. She looked young and sweet. People always wanted to help her. This was a mistake. Tracey looked like a doll, but she was very good at looking after herself. She was clever, and could have any job she wanted. But when Tracey was very young, she discovered that being pretty meant that she could have what she wanted without ever working for it.

I wonder what the wedding dress will be like? When Andy's mother took all my measurements, she said it would be a surprise. I think she wanted me to be more interested, but I don't care. I just hope it's something from a designer shop. I'll be able to sell it later.

When I told Andy's parents I had no family and no money, they felt so sorry for me. Well, it was true that I have no money. If I'm lucky, they will never find out that I have a grandmother, a mother and father and two sisters. Anyway, even if they do find out, it won't change anything. I'll be married to their son and spending his money.

Earlier in the year, Tracey was living with her grandmother in an apartment owned by the city. Her grandmother was old and sick. It was Tracey's job to look after her. The city paid her some money because she was taking care of her grandmother. Her parents gave her money as well. Tracey spent almost all her money on clothes. She did nothing to help her grandmother. The old lady did everything for Tracey. Often Tracey wasn't even there. She had a boyfriend, Danny. He lived in an empty office building with six other people. They slept on the floor, and mostly ate takeaways. They spent their time playing computer games and hacking into websites. Tracey thought hacking would be a good way to make money easily. When Tracey was interested in something, she could work very hard. Danny taught her everything he knew. Tracey learnt a lot from him. She was smarter than Danny, so she was soon better at hacking than him or his friends. She thought they could use their computer skills to steal money, but they were not interested. When they broke the security of the tax department, and read the tax information of thousands of people, they just posted notices on Facebook and Twitter saying how clever they were. Tracey thought they were crazy. She saw there were ways to get a lot of money, without working. "People who work for money are stupid," she told Danny. "If you are smart, you can have everything you want without ever having a job."

Tracey had found a way to transfer money between bank accounts. The problem was, that she could only move small amounts into her secret bank account. People didn't notice small amounts, but if large sums went missing from their personal bank accounts, they would start asking questions. Tracey didn't want the police to catch her. She couldn't use Danny's computer for this, because in many ways he was a very honest person. She had a fake student ID, so she used the university's computers. One day she was using a computer in the library, when a young man sitting at the next computer spoke to her. "Damn. This computer isn't working for me. I want to send some files, but I can't do it. I'm not familiar with this system. Are you having any problems?"

"No," said Tracey. She continued typing.

The man got out of his chair and came to stand behind her.

"You are really quick," he said. "What are you working on? Are you a computer science student?"

"Yes," lied Tracey. "I'm working on a program for my professor. Could you go away?"

"I'm sure you can fix my problem." The man didn't go away. "If you fix it so that I can send these files, I'll buy you lunch."

Tracey thought about it. She was tired of takeaways and her grandmother's cooking.

"OK," she said. "But you have to take me to a nice restaurant."

That was how it began. Andy had finished his PhD. He had a research position at the university. He had his own office. He was only in the library that day because his computer was in the repair shop. Tracey started visiting him in his office. Andy believed she was a student. He let her use his computer. After a month, she told him she had to move out of her apartment. She told him that the girls she lived with were not nice to her. She moved into Andy's apartment. He had a spare bedroom. He paid for everything. Tracey could not believe how easy it was.

In the summer, Andy told her that he had got a job at a university in Italy. "I'm very lucky," he told her. "I speak Italian, and I like Italy a lot. I'm going to leave here at Christmas and start my new job in January. Perhaps when you have finished your studies you can come and visit me there."

Tracey was angry. "Why don't you take me?" she asked.

Andy was very surprised. "But Tracey, you must finish your studies. I am sure you can find a new apartment to share with nice girls. You must have been able to save money while you have been living here."

Tracey did not want the situation to change. She thought about it. Danny had a new girlfriend, and Tracey didn't want to go back to live with her grandmother. Andy seemed to be rich. He had a nice apartment, and expensive clothes. He had a big car. He was happy to take Tracey to the pub and to good restaurants. He never asked her to pay for anything. Every week he went to visit his parents. He told her they had a very big house, and a garden with a tennis court. He talked about his Uncle James, who was a diplomat.

It would be a good idea to marry him, she thought. *He believes everything I tell him and he never asks questions. I will be able to do anything I like. His family is rich.*

Tracey found it was very easy to persuade Andy that he loved her, and that he could not go to Italy without her.

"Tracey! May we come in?"

Tracey went and opened the bedroom door. Andy's mother came in, followed by another woman who was carrying a huge white bundle.

"This is Mrs Meadows, the village dressmaker. She has been working on the family wedding dress," said Andy's mother.

"The family wedding dress?" Tracey was puzzled. "I thought you were going to buy me a dress."

"Oh no, dear. This is much better. My mother wore this dress, and then I wore it. It came from a famous fashion house. Of course, in those days the family was very wealthy, so my mother could afford to have a famous fashion house like Worth make a dress for her. The lace is beautiful. You are a bit bigger than I was when I got married, but Mrs Meadows has taken the sleeves out and used the material to make the top bigger. We just have to check that it fits well."

8. PUBLIC ENEMY NUMBER 1

On Friday morning, David Carver, the head of MI6, met with his senior staff.

"Can you tell me why James Winchester has become public enemy number 1?" he asked.

"We got information that he was involved in selling arms to terrorists," said Bevan Jenkins, the chief analyst. "We think that Simon Birley found out. So Winchester arranged to have him killed."

"Where did the information come from?" asked the boss.

"From the CIA," answered Bevan.

"What department in the CIA?"

"Uh. We don't know. It just came in a coded email from a general address."

"And you believed it?"

"We checked, of course, but no one we asked at the CIA could tell us more. They asked us to give them all the information we have, but we don't have any.

"Then the French and German security service contacted us. They had heard that James Winchester had been seen meeting with some Russians in Rome. These Russians are members of the group that sells materials for making nuclear weapons. The French and Germans asked us for more information too. We didn't have any, but they said that the information about Winchester came from here. From MI6."

"This is ridiculous," said Carver. "Everyone is hearing things and passing them on, but no one knows the source of the information. I would be very happy if you would concentrate on finding out who killed Simon Birley, and why."

"So you don't think James Winchester is involved? Shall we stop looking for him?" The chief analyst was surprised.

"I didn't say that. I don't know what the connection is, but Simon and James were very close friends. And James is now missing. Have you thought that he might have been kidnapped too? Or maybe murdered?"

"Yes, we thought about that. But the Italian police told us he had been seen near his apartment after Simon Birley's body was found. Everyone seems to think that Winchester is still alive, and is either on the run, or is in hiding."

"Who is 'everyone'?"

"Oh, the CIA, the French, the Italians, the Russians. Even the Chinese sent a message to say they would watch out for him, and help us in any way they could."

"That's nice of them. Do they know something we don't?" Carver was worried. He knew James very well. He didn't believe any of the stories, but he couldn't ignore them. Something was happening, but he didn't know what it was, and neither did any of his staff.

"Keep on looking for James, but don't believe everything our friends in other countries are telling us. When we find him, perhaps he will be able to solve the mystery. Have you any new information, Neil?"

"We are getting information from the police all the time. But it's all useless," said the operations manager, Neil Gillespie. "The problem is that the public saw Winchester's picture on television and in the newspapers. The police are getting hundreds of reports from people who think they have seen him. They tell us, and then the police send people, and we send people too, to check the reports. It's taking a lot of time. All of this would be easier if the television and newspapers weren't getting so much information."

"I agree. Where are they getting it from?"

"The news agencies say most of the information is coming from the Italian police, but the Italians say they are not talking to the media."

"Well, someone is giving them information," said Bevan Jenkins.

"I wish it would stop." Neil Gillespie sounded angry. "It's like trying to do your job on a TV reality show."

"So, can you tell me anything that is a fact, rather than a rumour?"

Carver asked his staff.

"Yes. Security cameras recorded someone who looked a lot like James Winchester at a highway café outside Rome. And Italian police picked up a signal from his mobile phone. They found the phone on a truck crossing the border from Italy into France but no Winchester." Neil Gillespie was pleased to be able to report something.

"That doesn't mean anything. If James Winchester put his phone on a truck going to France, then we know that he is not in France."

The Head of MI6 was correct. James was not in France, he had just arrived in Ireland.

9. A TRIP TO IRELAND

From Alberto's house, the car moved out of the streets of Rome and onto the motorway. Five hours later, the driver took an exit and drove through the outskirts of Milan. He turned into a car park attached to some offices.

"I'll leave you here," said the driver. "Your next driver is waiting in the office for you."

James got out of the car. The driver turned the car around and sped away. Carrying his bags, James walked towards the office. Most of the building was in darkness. There was just one light on in a room near the main entrance.

I hope this isn't a trap, he thought.

As he got close to the building, the main door opened.

"Come in here," a voice whispered.

James went in.

"Hurry!" whispered the voice again. A man in the dark hallway took James' arm and pushed him into the room with the light on.

"I am Nino. Put these on over your clothes, and put your bags in this box. We have to get there by 3:00am."

The man handed James a pair of overalls and a cap. The box had Allia-Euro Cargo Services Express printed on the side, and a company logo. The same logo was on the overalls and cap. James saw that the man was dressed the same way.

"Quickly! I'll take the box." James and Nino ran to a small truck waiting in the yard.

Nino drove very fast.

"We must get to the airfield by 3:00am. at the latest. The plane won't wait for us."

"What plane?" asked James.

"Your ride to Ireland," was the surprising reply. "When we get to the airport, I will take you to the cargo area. There will be someone there to tell you what to do."

A cargo plane was parked waiting at the airfield. Nino drove directly to a large shed. It was a very busy place. He drove the car into the middle of the shed, stopped and wound down his window.

"Louis!" he shouted. "Louis! I have a last-minute courier package. "Can you put it on the plane? I have all the paperwork."

A very large man appeared. "The courier bags are sealed. You are too late!"

"But this is very special and important!" answered Nino. He handed an envelope to Louis.

"Oh. One of those packages," said Louis. "I hope he has good ID. The security in Ireland's a lot tougher these days."

"He's one of Alberto's," explained Nino.

"It should be all right then. OK. But hurry, we don't have much time."

"Get out and go with Louis," Nino told James.

James got out with the box containing the suitcase. Louis took the box. He pointed to an open truck. James climbed in, and Louis lifted the box onto the truck. He then climbed into the driver's seat, and they set off across the tarmac to the waiting plane.

Louis stopped the truck next to the plane. Two men in uniforms were standing chatting near the front of the plane. A third man was throwing packets and bags in through an open cargo door.

"You have 24 hours off," Louis told the man who was loading the plane. "This man's going to do your job. You'll still get paid."

The man nodded. "I'll just finish loading," he said.

The two men in uniforms said nothing, but one of them waved his hand towards the cargo door.

James and Louis climbed into the plane. Louis pointed to a row of seats against the inside wall. "You won't be comfortable, but you'll get to Ireland."

James sat on one of the seats. One of the pilots climbed in through the cargo door and handed James some ear plugs. "You'll need these," he said. "I'm Guido. The chief pilot's called Santi. When we land in Ireland, we will have to wait by the plane until our papers are checked. I hope your papers are in order. Do you have a passport?"

Yes," said James. "What are you going to tell them about me?"

Guido smiled. "The cargo handlers in Ireland are terrible. We need to have a fast turn-around, so we bring our own man to help with unloading and loading the plane. That will be you. You will have to do some work. What's your name?"

"Lorenzo Morelli," answered James.

"Sure. I don't believe that. But it doesn't matter. The people in Ireland will believe you, I hope. I'll go and change the name on the paperwork."

He went away.

The flight to Dublin took about two hours. It was dark inside the cargo area of the plane. James tried to sleep, but it was impossible. He couldn't wait for the flight to end. His face was tight from the glue Alicia had used around his mouth and eyes. The plugs inside his nose made it difficult to breathe. He couldn't risk rubbing his face, or taking the plugs out. The officials in Ireland would look at his face and his passport picture. He must look like the picture.

Finally they landed in Ireland. After about twenty minutes, someone came and opened the cargo door. James climbed out. He was very stiff. The sun was up. The light hurt his eyes. He had been sitting in the dark for more than two hours.

He stood by the side of the plane and waited.

I must remember not to speak English, he thought. *I am Lorenzo Morelli from the south of Italy.*

The immigration and customs men came in a black van and checked Guido and Santi's papers. "Where's the third man?" they asked.

"He's over there," answered Guido.

Guido waved to James, and James walked over.

"Why do you bring an extra person?" asked the immigration official. Guido explained about needing extra help to unload the plane.

"Do you have a passport?" he asked James. James handed it over, and held his breath. The immigration official looked at him, and then looked at his passport photograph.

"You look a lot older than your picture," he said. James didn't answer.

"He doesn't speak English," said Guido.

"You look a lot older than the photograph in your passport," the immigration official repeated in Italian.

"Oh," answered James in a strong southern Italian accent. "I didn't sleep at all last night."

The man laughed, and handed back his passport. "If you want a job like this, you will have to get used to it."

The customs and immigration men walked away. Then James started to help unload the plane. It was only a few minutes before Guido came over and said, "Our return trip is delayed. One of our landing lights is broken. They're sending someone to replace it, but they can't get here until 10:00. So we're going to a hotel to get a good breakfast. There's nothing much to eat here. You can come with us if you like."

James nodded. He took his bags out of the box, and followed Guido and Santi to the front of the freight building.

There were trucks and vans everywhere. One of the van drivers called out to them.

"Do you want a ride into town? I'm leaving now."

"Can you take three of us?" shouted back Guido.

"Sure."

The friendly van driver drove them to the nearby town. He stopped the van outside a small hotel near the railway station.

"How far are we from the centre of Dublin?" asked James as the van drove away.

"About 40km," answered Guido. "You can catch a train. But I guess you want to get something to eat first. Come with us. This is the best breakfast in Ireland."

The hotel restaurant was next to the lobby. It had a sign on the door 'Dublin fry up'.

"You get bacon, sausages, eggs, everything…," said Santi speaking for the first time.

They went into the restaurant and sat down. It was now almost 7:30. They ordered three Dublin fry ups and coffee.

"I need to go to the bathroom," said Guido. "I will be back soon." He walked towards the door of the restaurant. As he walked, James saw him taking his mobile phone from his pocket.

Something is not right, thought James. *That guy is too helpful and friendly.*

When I was a spy, I sometimes got this feeling about danger. I have it now.

He stood up. "I have to go to the bathroom too. And I want to change my clothes," he told the other man.

Santi just nodded.

James took his bags and went out of the restaurant. The lobby of the hotel was empty. Then he saw Guido on the street, just outside the door. He had his back to the hotel, and was talking into his phone. Guido was speaking loudly in English. James could hear him clearly.

"I don't know who he is, but he is running away from someone. He came to us from a man called Alberto. Alberto's service is very expensive, so this man has a lot of money, or very powerful friends. I am sure you, the police, would want him. When you have him, you can find out who he is. I will tell you where he is, if you pay me..."

James decided he needed to move quickly. He found the back door of the hotel.

I knew there was something wrong. But there's one good thing. Guido doesn't know who I am, he thought.

James hurried to the railway station. He went into the men's room there, and took off the overalls and cap. He was still wearing the clothes Alberto had brought from Lorenzo Morelli. He washed his face carefully so that he didn't disturb the glue around his mouth and eyes. He tidied his hair. He needed a shave, but he couldn't worry about that now.

He took a train towards Dublin.

I should keep moving. But I have to eat and sleep. If I don't get some sleep, I'll make a mistake, he thought.

After two stations, James got off the train. He bought sandwiches and water at a small shop near the railway station. He found a small hotel in a quiet street. When he got to his room, he ate and drank a little, took the plugs out of his nose and got into the bed. Just as he fell asleep, he realized that he had left Alberto's house only twelve hours ago. It seemed a lot longer.

When James woke up it was dark. He looked at the clock next to the bed. He had been asleep for ten hours. He felt dirty and very hungry, but at least he was not so tired.

He took a long shower, shaved, and changed his clothes. He looked at the rest of the sandwiches he had bought at the railway station.

I don't feel like eating those. I'm going to go out and have a good meal. I'm not even going to change my face, he thought.

It was strange, but most of the restaurants in the town were Italian. *I really don't feel like Italian food,* he thought. Finally he found a steak bar. It was very crowded and noisy. He ate oysters. Then he ordered steak. No one looked at him. Everyone was too busy eating and drinking. *It's true that the best place to hide is in public view,* James smiled to himself.

Back at the hotel, James lay on the bed and thought about what to do next. He wanted to go to Britain, but where? He wanted to talk to someone, but who could he talk to? He would like to talk to Archie Ross. But if the police were also looking for him, that would be a mistake. Archie Ross was a very senior policeman. Even if Archie wanted to help James, he couldn't. James thought about Sarah. He wondered what she was doing. He wished that he and Sarah were eating dinner together in the hotel in London. *Tomorrow is Andy's wedding,* he thought. *Well, I won't be there. I wonder if Sarah will go without me? She knows Andy well, and she likes him. So maybe she will go alone.*

For some reason this made James feel very lonely. *Don't be so stupid,* he told himself. *You have a problem to solve here. Your love life will have to wait for a while.*

10. NEXT MORNING

James left the hotel early the next morning. He took a train into the centre of Dublin. He ate a large breakfast at a café on Grafton Street. By nine o'clock, the streets were full of Saturday shoppers. He went to a camping store and bought a backpack, walking boots, jeans, and a waterproof jacket. He also bought sunglasses, a wool hat, a torch, and some fishing equipment. James wanted to look like a tourist on a walking and fishing holiday. He found an empty park, and transferred his shopping, and everything from the suitcase and the airline travel bag, to the backpack. He hid the bags in some bushes. He felt much better with the backpack. It was easier to move around, and he would be able to run if necessary. Then he went to an electrical store, and bought a memory stick. He walked through the streets until he found an Internet café. He had taken Simon's memory stick from his belt. He paid for an hour's computer time, and looked at Simon's memory stick for the first time. Four folders had been saved to the memory stick. They were all named The Finders Market, but had different dates: 1954-1974; 1975-1995; 1996-2004; 2005-present.

He didn't open the folders and look at the files, but he wondered what they meant. He quickly copied the files onto the new memory stick, and signed off. He then went to a nearby stationery shop and bought a padded envelope.

Next James found a hotel. He went to the front desk, and took a room using Lorenzo Morelli's credit card. Once he was in the room, he called a courier company to come and collect a package. He wrote an address on the envelope he had bought that morning. He planned to send the memory stick to Archie Ross. The envelope was marked 'personal and confidential' and was addressed to Archie at Edinburgh Central Police Station. Archie was an old friend, and he had known Simon Birley well. Archie might not be able to help James, but Archie would take good care of the memory stick and the data on it. Archie would know what to do with the information.

He went into the bathroom, and put the nose plugs back in. He used the glue Alicia had given him to change the shape of his eyes and mouth. He didn't want the courier to recognise him as James Winchester.

The courier came, and James filled out the paperwork and paid him. He used Lorenzo Morelli's name, and gave the hotel as the sender's address.

Then James lay down on the bed and forced himself to relax. The most difficult part was still to come.

Late in the afternoon he ordered a meal from room service. After he ate, he prepared to leave. He planned to take the ferry from Dublin to Holyhead in Wales. James' brother–in–law, Tom Fairweather, owned a small cottage on the coast, not far from the ferry terminal. The cottage had belonged to Tom's great uncle. Like James, Tom was a keen fisherman. The two of them had often spent fishing weekends there in the summer, but the cottage was not often used at other times of the year. It was only about 8km from Holyhead, but it was very isolated. James planned to go there and stay for a few days.

He would have to travel as Lorenzo Morelli. He hoped he wouldn't be recognized, and that no one knew what name he was using. He thought about Guido. Had Guido given the police the name? The name was on the cargo plane paperwork but he didn't think Guido would have given the police much information. Not until they paid him. Would the police pay Guido for the information he was offering?

He couldn't be sure, but he would have to take the risk. He planned to take an evening ferry, and then walk from Holyhead to the cottage. It would only take a couple of hours.

James emptied everything out of the backpack. He searched through Lorenzo Morelli's clothes, and chose a shirt and a pair of casual trousers. He put the rest of the clothes into a hotel laundry bag.

He unpacked the fishing equipment he had bought. The most important item was a knife. It was bigger than a knife a fisherman would normally use, but James hoped that if his bag was searched, nobody would notice. He would rather have a gun, but a knife was better than nothing. He hoped he wouldn't have to use it. He put the boots, shorts, hat and jacket into the backpack, along with his shaving gear.

He spent a long time in the bathroom working on his face, as Alicia had taught him. The final result was not as good as she had done, but he hoped it would be good enough. He collected all the packaging and paper and took it down to the basement of the hotel, where he found some garbage cans. He took the laundry bag too, and hid it behind a washing machine in the hotel laundry. If anyone found it, they would think it belonged to a guest.

Then he went back upstairs, collected his backpack and checked out.

The trip to Holyhead was very easy. James walked to the ferry port. He stopped at a crowded pub, and changed into his walking clothes and boots in the men's restroom. No one noticed that a man went into the toilets wearing a shirt and trousers, and came out dressed in walking clothes.

He bought a ticket for the last ferry of the day. It was a slow ferry, and would take more than three hours. James hoped that the security men at Holyhead would be tired and want to go home. Perhaps they would not look at his passport too closely.

On board the ferry, James found a seat in the lounge. He bought sandwiches and a cup of coffee. There were very few passengers. He felt very tired, but he couldn't risk going to sleep. He watched a replay of a football match on the television and listened to a group of young men on their way home from a friend's wedding in Dublin. They were very loud, and very drunk. They were watching the football match on TV as well. They shouted a lot at the referee.

The ferry arrived in Holyhead just after midnight. James felt worried as he got off the boat. The security gate was very brightly lit, and there seemed to be people in uniforms everywhere.

It was too late now. He would have to risk it. He followed the wedding guests. Perhaps they would cause trouble and no one would notice him.

James was very lucky. Just as he got to the gate carrying his passport, one of the young men climbed up the security wall. His friends cheered. Men in uniforms ran towards the wall. The man climbed higher, and sat on top of the wall, singing. Then, very slowly, he fell backwards and disappeared. There was a shout and a loud bang as he landed on the wharf below. His friends clapped and shouted.

"Idiots," said the man on the gate. "As if we haven't got enough trouble."

"Trouble?" asked James in a very strong Italian accent.

"We're on high security alert. Everyone's looking for an English diplomat, who has gone mad and joined a terrorist group. I don't know why they think he would come here."

He opened Lorenzo Morelli's passport, but he hardly looked at James. He was too interested in the drama happening behind James. Several other members of the group were now trying to climb the wall.

"Have a nice vacation, Mr Morelli," he said handing the passport back to James. James could not believe his luck. He forced himself to move slowly through the gate as the immigration official shouted "Next!"

Outside the ferry terminal James started walking along the coast.

11. TRACEY IS ANGRY

Tracey was in a bad mood. She was in the car with Andy. She had not enjoyed the wedding. Everyone said she looked very beautiful. That was nice. But people always told Tracey she was beautiful, so that was nothing special.

The day had not started well. Tracey had told Andy's parents she had no family and no friends. So Andy's mother had asked one of Andy's cousins, Megan, to be bridesmaid. She was a tall cheerful young woman. At first Tracey was pleased. Megan was not very pretty, so Tracey didn't have to worry about competition. But Megan talked a lot, and asked difficult questions.

She came in the morning to help Tracey get dressed. The hairdresser, make up specialist, and manicurist arrived too. Andy's mother was paying for everything. It should have been very nice. But then Megan asked, "What are you going to give Andy as a wedding gift?"

Tracey was surprised. She was the bride. Andy should give her a present. But she had never even thought that she should give him anything.

"Nothing," she answered Megan. "I don't have any money."

Megan was amazed. "Oh, of course. I know. You have no family, and you are a student. But surely you bought him some little thing. Or made him something?"

"Made? What would I make him?"

"Oh, I don't know. An embroidery? A very special card, or letter?"

Tracey was angry. She never did anything for anyone else, but she didn't like people noticing that.

"Andy has bought you a present," said Megan. "I know. I heard him talking to his father about it. His father said it was too expensive, but Andy said 'she will be my wife. I want to buy her something special'."

Tracey felt happier. *Good! I wonder what the present is. Jewellery?* she thought.

She was sure that Megan would sympathise with her, so she said. "You know, I feel very embarrassed."

"Why?" Megan was interested.

"Well, Andy's mother said she would give me a wedding dress. But she didn't. I feel bad, because all she did was get an old wedding dress altered for me. No one wants to get married in a second-hand dress."

"It's not a second-hand dress! It's a family treasure. And the lace in the wedding dress – it's priceless! It's a very valuable dress and I've always dreamed of wearing it," said Megan.

Tracey still felt angry, but then she thought, *That lace is priceless, and the dress is very valuable. Good! Maybe I can still sell it.*

Tracey looked like a princess in the dress. Mrs Meadows had done a wonderful job. Andy was very proud when he saw her at the ceremony. "You look so beautiful," he said.

Tracey smiled at him. *He is an idiot,* she thought. *But at least he has money.*

Everyone at the wedding told her she looked wonderful, and that Andy was very lucky. There was just one woman who didn't seem to like Tracey. She was very thin, with white hair. Her blue silk dress was very elegant, and fitted her perfectly. She was wearing sapphire and diamond earrings, and a matching necklace. Tracey knew a lot about clothes. She knew that the woman's dress had been expensive, and she guessed the jewellery was real.

It was strange. The woman didn't seem to know anyone, only Andy. Andy ran towards her when he saw her, and they hugged and kissed. Later he said, "That's my Uncle James' friend, Sarah. She's great!"

Tracey thought it would be good to make friends with Sarah. She must have a lot of money, and Tracey knew that Andy's Uncle James was rich. James was in trouble with the police, but no one was talking about it. Andy and Andy's mother said it was a big mistake, and she wasn't to worry about it.

Of course, Tracey wasn't worried. She wondered if the police would shoot him. That would be good. James had no wife, and no children. So maybe if James died, Andy would get his money. But nothing was certain. If it was a mistake, Andy's Uncle James would reappear. If that happened, the best thing would be for Tracey to be friends with Sarah.

She went to talk to Sarah. Sarah was very pleasant and polite. Tracey smiled and looked cute, and talked about having no family, but Sarah just smiled politely and didn't say anything.

Then there had been the wedding present from Andy. He had bought her a computer. Tracey was not happy. She expected jewellery, not a computer!

"I thought you would like to have your own computer. So when we are in Italy you can keep studying. Of course I know you will want to get a job. I talked to the university. If you can finish your degree, they have jobs in the computer science department. It will be wonderful!"

Tracey smiled at Andy and thanked him sweetly. *He thinks I want a job. I'm not going to work! Why does he think I married him?*

The last disaster of the day had been the dress. Tracey was changing out of the wedding dress when Andy's mother arrived.

"I'll take the dress now, dear. So you won't be worried about it on your honeymoon," she said.

"I don't mind. I can easily take care of it," answered Tracey. She planned to put the dress up for sale on-line as soon as possible.

"No," said Andy's mother. "I'll take it and get it cleaned so it's ready for the next bride. One of Andy's friends was talking to Megan a lot. So maybe she will be next. Of course she is very tall. I wonder what Mrs Meadows can do to make it longer."

"But it's my dress!" shouted Tracey.

Andy's mother looked surprised. "You're tired, dear. It's been a long day. It's not your dress. It's a family dress. I'll take it now."

Andy's mother waited until Tracey had changed, and then she took the dress away.

Two hours later Tracey was still in a bad mood.

"Where are we going?" she asked Andy.

"It's a surprise," he answered. "You are going to love it. I have planned something very special for our honeymoon."

"But I'm tired. When will we get there?"

"Mmm," Andy said. "I'm sorry. It will take us about another three hours. Why don't you sleep?"

Tracey was about to start shouting. Then she thought, *It will be one of those very expensive country house hotels. That will be nice.*

"OK, darling," she said. "Maybe I will sleep a little. Please wake me up when we get there. I'm looking forward to the surprise."

12. THE FINDERS MARKET

While James was walking along the windy coastline of Wales towards the fishing cottage, and Andy was driving along the M6 motorway, a group of men were holding an audio conference. Their voices were distorted by voice-changing software, and they were using a secure server.

They belonged to a group called the 'Finders Market'. Only one member, the 'Shop Keeper', knew who the other members were. Of course, the members were all in similar professions, so it was sometimes possible to guess that a colleague, or even an enemy from another country, might also belong to the group. But it was never possible to know for sure. All the members knew that if they ever did anything that would endanger the group, they would immediately be killed. Of course it would look like an accident, or suicide, but they would be dead just the same.

In the sixty-year history of the Finders Market, killings of current members had been rare. The members were very carefully selected. They were professionals and had been very highly trained by their different countries. They did not make mistakes.

The members communicated only with the Shop Keeper. In the history of the Finders Market, there had only been five Shop Keepers. No one knew who the Shop Keeper was, or where he or she lived. It might be in the Caribbean, the Pacific, the jungles of Vietnam, or in the centre of Athens.

The Shop Keeper communicated with the group members individually.

A meeting like this one was very unusual. But the situation was serious. An Englishman, Simon Birley, had spent almost twenty years investigating the group. No one had known this. He had not told anyone what he was doing. He had quietly and carefully gathered data and analysed it. He had hacked into files and communications without anyone finding out. He had always covered his tracks. One thing was clear, Simon Birley had been much cleverer and more skilful than anyone realized. It seemed that he had developed an image of a quiet, friendly team worker with no special skills, to hide what he was doing.

The Chinese were developing advanced hacking skills to monitor and disrupt other countries' intelligence databases. A group based in Beijing was testing a spy worm by hacking into the Spanish army's stores and purchase department records. When their software met another spy worm 'face to face', for that millisecond, the spy worms were connected. The Chinese hackers thought it was funny. They were meeting their counterparts in the spy game. They made jokes about the worms being male and female, a love match, but they also reported it to their supervisor. The supervisor told his boss, Zhang, who was a member of the Finder's Market.

"It was very strange," said the supervisor. "Our group traced the other worm to the British Council in Rome. I guess there is some smart young person there playing games. Maybe they practice hacking in their lunch hours."

"I'm sure you are right," answered Zhang. "But tell your group to be very careful. If they could locate the other hacker, then the other hacker could also track them."

As soon as the other man left the room, Zhang told his secretary that he had a stomach problem, and was going home. She called for his car and driver. Zhang's wife and household staff came running out of the house to meet him, but he ignored them. He went to his private office. He opened a hidden safe, and took out a very sophisticated mini-computer. He sent a coded message to the Shop Keeper.

It's always best to be careful, he thought.

Only the Shop Keeper and Zhang knew this part of the story. The Shop Keeper ordered an investigation of Simon Birley through an English member of the group. The results had shocked the Shop Keeper. He had ordered the investigation because he liked to be careful, but he hadn't believed that Simon Birley had discovered anything important. No one before had ever found out about the group, or their activities.

Even now, the Shop Keeper did not think that Simon Birley had found out very much. But the situation was dangerous. He had sent an order to the English member to arrange for Simon Birley to be taken. After they found out how much he knew, he could be killed.

This had only been partly successful. It was possible that Simon Birley had passed some information to James Winchester. And James Winchester could not be found.

Through their positions and their connections, the group could activate the intelligence services and the police of twenty countries. They had created stories, lies, and rumours. Everyone was looking for James, but he had escaped.

Each member reported what he or she had been doing to catch James Winchester. Some members agreed that their countries would combine to spread stories of terrorism and bombs. It would be impossible for him to escape.

"We need more effort," said the Shop Keeper. "We don't know how much this James Winchester knows, but even if he guesses something, we are all in danger. Also, while we are hunting for this man, we can't carry out our normal business. Do anything you have to do. Find a way to persuade your police and secret service to kill him as soon as they see him. We must fix this problem."

13. CLOGWYN COTTAGE

It was easy to walk along the coast to the cottage. James used the tourist walking-track. He had his torch, and there was a full moon. It was almost 2:30am when he arrived. The cottage was made from stone. It was tiny; just one large room, with two windows and a door facing the sea, with a small kitchen and bathroom at the back. A shed behind the house was used to store fishing nets and garden furniture. The two buildings were between two low hills. In front of the cottage the ground sloped towards a steep rock cliff. To the south, there were some steps going down to a beach with some old buildings and a small wharf.

James stopped on the hill above the cottage and listened carefully. Everything was quiet. There was no sign of life. He noticed that the grass around the cottage had been cut.

Perhaps Tom pays someone to keep the cottage and garden tidy, he thought.

He looked out along the coast towards the beach. Many years ago, the old buildings had been a fish-canning factory. The wharf looked different. Last time James had been here, it had been falling down, but it seemed to have been repaired. There was a new road too. James could see it on the hill in the distance.

It must be fifteen years since I last came here. Of course things have changed. I hope the key is in the same place, he thought.

He walked down the hill towards the cottage. He stretched up and ran his hand along a window frame. His fingers found the small hole where the key was hidden.

He unlocked the door, and walked into the main room of the

cottage.

He stopped, amazed, and dropped his backpack on the floor. The cottage looked completely different from what he remembered.

Maybe Tom sold it? No. Tom doesn't use the cottage much now, but he spent a lot of his childhood here. He loved it. He would never sell it, thought James.

James looked around. There was a double bed at one end of the room. The pale blue and white striped bed coverings looked new. There were candles and flowers. A sign hanging over the bed said 'Happy honeymoon!'

Oh no! James suddenly understood. *Andy is spending his honeymoon here! That's bad luck. Let's see. It is after 2:30am now. The wedding was yesterday, Saturday. If they drove here after the wedding, they could arrive at any moment. I'll hide in the shed, but I need something to eat and drink first.*

He went into the kitchen and switched on the light. He opened the old-fashioned refrigerator. It was full of delicious food, champagne and wine. He looked in the cupboards. He took a packet of crackers from one of the cupboards, some cheese and a bottle of orange juice from the refrigerator. He turned off the light, picked up his backpack, and went back out the front door.

James locked the door, and put the key back in its hiding place.

The shed behind the cottage was not locked. By the light of his torch, James found a long garden chair and a box of old blankets.

He ate his meal, then made a pillow from his jacket, pulled some blankets over himself, and lay down to sleep. He took the knife out of his backpack and put it under his pillow.

James heard Andy's car arrive. *I will leave as soon as I can,* he thought *They'll never know I was here.*

Andy didn't wake Tracey when they arrived at the cottage. She looked beautiful asleep. People said that she looked like an angel, and Andy thought it was true.

Her parents would have loved the wedding. *Pity they're dead,* he thought.

He got the key, unlocked the door, and carried their bags into the cottage. Then he went back.

"Wake up, darling, we're here."

"Where?" Tracey looked out the car window. "Where are we?"

"My honeymoon surprise for you. It's perfect. We will be completely alone. It's a very romantic place."

"But where are we staying?"

Andy moved so that Tracey could see the cottage. "In the cottage. It's very old and small. Perfect for just two people."

"That!" Tracey shouted. "People stay in hotels for honeymoons! Not in dirty old cottages in the middle of nowhere!"

"It's very comfortable. And my mother paid a woman from the village to clean, and make up the bed, and bring food in. You'll see. It will be perfect."

"How long are we supposed to stay here?"

"I thought we could stay a week. Then we will have to go back and start packing to go to Italy."

"A week! What am I going to do here for a week?"

"There is a beach. We can walk and look for shells. The fishing's good too. There's no telephone and no mobile phone connection. No one will bother us. It will be wonderful. Just the two of us."

"I'm not staying here. Take me to a hotel."

Andy looked at Tracey. She did not look beautiful now. She looked bad tempered and ugly.

"I'm sorry. I'm sorry you don't like my surprise. But I'm not taking you to a hotel now. I have been driving for more than five hours, and I'm tired. We will stay here tonight."

Tracey was surprised. Andy never said 'no' to her.

She got out of the car, and walked into the cottage. She picked up her bag, and found the bathroom. When she reappeared she was wearing a nightdress. Andy tried to give her a glass of champagne.

Tracey ignored him. "I don't know where you are going to sleep, but you are not sleeping in this bed with me." She reached up and pulled the 'happy honeymoon' sign off the wall and threw it on the floor. Then she got into the bed and turned her face towards the wall.

Andy was very upset and disappointed.

He found a blanket in an old wooden chest at the end of the bed. Then he took a pillow from the bed and went out to the car. A second later he came back, and took the bottle of champagne. *Might as well drink it,* he thought.

Andy spent the rest of his wedding night sitting in his car, drinking champagne. He saw the sunrise. It was beautiful. The rays from the sun travelled across the roof of the cottage where his very angry new wife was sleeping. For a short time the tiny house looked golden.

This was a bad idea. I thought she would love it. Perhaps she will be happier after a long sleep. If not, I guess I will have to take her to a hotel. I wonder if I can afford it?

Finally, as the sun climbed into the sky, he fell asleep.

14. WHAT ARE YOU DOING HERE?

It was almost lunchtime when Andy woke up. His neck and back were hurting. He climbed out of the car and went into the cottage. He found some clothes and took a shower. Tracey had been up. She had eaten croissants for breakfast. There was milk spilt on the counter, an open packet of butter, and croissant crumbs on the floor. He looked over to the bed. She was lying facing the wall, with the covers pulled up over her head.

Shall I try talking to her? he wondered. *No,* he decided. He was stiff after sleeping in the car. Perhaps he had made a mistake choosing the cottage for a honeymoon, but she was being very unfriendly.

I don't like her very much right now, he thought. He turned the coffee maker on, cleaned the kitchen counter and the floor, and collected food for a gourmet picnic. He put everything on a tray and went back outside.

Andy put the tray on the bonnet of the car and went to the shed. He wanted the picnic table and chairs. He planned to eat his meal in comfort.

Andy was not sure what happened next. He opened the door. The shed was dark. He saw a long garden chair and a pile of blankets. The next moment, there was a knife against his throat, and a voice saying, "Don't move."

The door was pulled shut, and a torch shone in Andy's face. "Oh, it's you, Andy. Sorry," said James.

James let go of Andy. Andy fell to the floor.

"James!" he said weakly. "What on earth are you doing here?"

"Hiding from the police and a lot of other people," answered James. "I'm sorry. I didn't think anyone would be here. When I realized the cottage was a honeymoon nest, I hid in here. I planned to leave as soon as it got dark again."

"I'm pleased you are OK," said Andy. "We have all been so worried. My mother is sure you were kidnapped. What can I do to help you?"

"I don't want you to do anything. I want you to stay out of this. It's dangerous."

"Why is it dangerous?"

"Some very unpleasant people are chasing me. They are using the police to search for me, and I am sure they know everything that the police know. If the police find me, these unpleasant people will kill me."

"Why? What did you do to them?"

"I didn't do anything. I have something they want."

"Well what is it? Why don't you give it to them?"

"It's not so simple. I don't know what it is. Even if I gave it to them, they would still kill me, because they think I know about it."

Andy found this hard to understand.

"You have something. But you don't know what it is. But the guys who are chasing you think you do know."

"Yes, that's right."

"So why can't you find out what you have? Then you might know who they are, and why they are chasing you. After all, they will kill you anyway."

James laughed. "You are quite right. It's better to be killed for what you know, than for what you don't know.

"The information is on computer files. I haven't looked at them, and I am sure they will be encrypted. I'm not good enough at computers to do things like that."

"No. Neither am I. But Tracey is."

"Your new wife? She is good with computers?"

"She's a computer science student. She specializes in computer security. She knows all about hackers and encryption and things like that."

"I don't think I can ask her. It will put her in danger too," said James.

"But who will know?" Andy argued. "I can ask her to look at the files. Maybe I don't even have to say that they came from you."

Andy didn't tell James that Tracey wasn't talking to him. It was too embarrassing.

James frowned. He didn't like it. But what choice did he have?

"OK," he said. "If you can think of a good story."

Just then the shed door opened. "Andy? Andy? Are you here? What are you doing?" Tracey had got bored. She thought perhaps Andy would agree to leave this horrible place now.

James moved against the wall where it was dark. Andy saw him slide the knife up his sleeve.

"Tracey! Are you feeling better?"

"Yes, darling. Do you think we could go to a hotel now? I stayed last night to please you. But I don't like it."

"No, Tracey. We can't leave yet. I have a job for you to do. You'll like it."

"What is it?"

"I have some computer files. They are probably encrypted. You are so clever at these things. I am sure you will be able to read them. It's important."

The shed door was wide open and light flooded into the space. Tracey saw the garden chair, the blankets and the backpack. Her mind worked very quickly.

"Your Uncle James is here isn't he? That's why you brought me here."

"No, no. I didn't know. James didn't know we were coming here."

"So he is here. Where is he?"

James gave up. He moved away from the wall and into the light.

"I am delighted to meet you at last, Tracey. Welcome to the family."

Andy stared. "James! What have you done to yourself?"

James was embarrassed. "I am a forty-year-old Italian called Lorenzo Morelli. You didn't think I could travel as myself, did you?"

"Why don't we go into the house?" asked Andy. "There's no reason for you to hide here now."

"OK," said James. "I would love to have a shower."

While James was taking his shower, Andy brought the tray back in from the garden. He made fresh coffee and laid out a meal on the table. Tracey was quiet. She was thinking. She decided she would not go to Italy with Andy. He was talking about small apartments and

Tracey getting a job. That was not in her plan. The marriage was a mistake. But if she left Andy, she would have no money. James was rich, and he was in trouble. The computer files were his. She knew she was clever, so she would find a way to make James give her some money.

James came into the room. He was wearing Morelli's shirt and trousers. He looked clean, and more like himself, but his hair was still black, and his eyebrows were different.

"You look more normal," said Andy. "But I think Sarah will get a shock when she sees you!"

"I get a shock every time I look in a mirror," answered James. He smiled, but Andy thought that his eyes looked sad.

He loves Sarah so much. It isn't fair that this happened. James just wanted a quiet life with her, Andy thought.

They ate lunch. Suddenly, Tracey was in a very good mood. She smiled and laughed. She told James that he was very handsome, and that she thought he was wonderful.

"I will do anything I can to help you. Are the computer files yours? I could look at them for you, but I would need a computer…"

"You have a computer!" Andy was very pleased. "Your wedding present!"

James was watching Tracey.

"Of course Andy! I didn't forget! It was such a wonderful present!" she said.

Andy cleared the food and plates off the table. He made more coffee. He went to the car and got the computer. He unpacked it and set it up on the table.

"Tracey," said James. "It is very nice of you to offer to help. But it is dangerous. Being in this cottage with me is dangerous. Looking at the files might make it worse. Are you sure you want to do this?"

I am clever. I can do this, and get all the money I want. The police never caught me before. I don't think they will catch me now. I am too smart for that, she thought.

"Oh. Please don't even think about it. I am Andy's wife. You are family. I want to do this for the family," said Tracey, in her girly voice.

James wasn't sure. But Andy was so pleased and proud, that James said nothing.

I'll be protecting her and Andy and trying not to get killed myself. At least Sarah is safe. At least, I hope she's safe, thought James.

James didn't believe that Tracey would be able to do much. She looked like a small pretty child. So he was surprised how expert she was when she sat down at the computer, inserted the memory stick and started looking at the files. She typed quickly, and started talking to herself.

After a while she said, "They are all encrypted. But the encryption is not the same. Some of the files in the folders with the earlier dates, 1954-1974, 1975-1995 and 1996-2004 will be easy to open and read. They're small, and were created nine or more years ago. I guess whoever made these files encrypted them at the same time. If the files weren't opened again, the encryption wasn't changed. All the later ones, '2005 to now' have newer and much more sophisticated protection. I don't think I can open those."

"So will you please open the easier ones?" asked James.

"I can't do it here. Computers don't come with decryption software already loaded. I will have to go somewhere with Internet access so that I can download the software I need."

"If you get the software, you'll be able to open at least some of the files?" asked James.

"Oh, yes. The software that people used ten years ago is now available to anyone who knows about these things. There's freeware. Some companies are still using that old style encryption, and then they wonder why hackers find it so easy to break into their systems."

"So I'll take you and the computer to somewhere that has Internet," said Andy. "The memory stick can stay here with James. You can get the software. We'll come back here, and we'll find out what's in the files."

Andy suggested they found an Internet Café in Holyhead, but Tracey didn't agree.

"A good hotel would be better," she said. "They always have WiFi connections, and if we book in as guests, I will be able to get everything I need in the privacy of our own room. That would be much safer than using an Internet café."

"Tracey!" said Andy. "It will cost too much!"

"No, Andy," said James. "Tracey has the right idea. You should go to a nice hotel, and book in as guests."

James thought that the police might be watching Andy and Tracey. It might look strange if they went to an Internet café on the first day of their honeymoon. But if they went and stayed in a good hotel, that would seem natural. Also, it might keep them out of danger for a while.

Andy still looked worried. "It's OK, Andy," said James. "I'll pay. Book in for three nights. Then when Tracey has everything she needs, have afternoon tea or a drink in the bar or something. So that people see you. Then say you are going out somewhere romantic for dinner."

Tracey was pleased with the plan. They would go to a good hotel. James would pay for everything.

"OK," she said. "But just now I need to make a list of the kind of software I need. It's hard to concentrate. Could you two please go for a walk or something? I'll come and find you when I've finished."

James and Andy went outside.

"I can't go for a walk," said James. "It's too risky. We don't know if the cottage is being watched. No one can see me between the cottage and the shed but I can't go any further. I'll wait in the shed. Why don't you go down to the beach?"

As soon as the two men left the room, Tracey copied the files from the memory stick onto the hard drive of the computer. She got changed and put on her make-up. She repacked her bags. Then she went out to find Andy. He was down on the beach near some old roofless buildings. She called to him, but he didn't hear her. Tracey had to go down the steps to the beach and shout again before he heard her.

He came running up to her.

"Have you finished? This beach is so beautiful. We will have to come back here. And they have fixed the old wharf because there is a wave energy project in the bay. You can see the turbines!"

Tracey didn't listen to him. "Come on, Andy. We don't have much time."

Andy put their luggage and the computer in the car. Tracey gave the memory stick back to James and they drove away.

Andy was in a very good mood. James had given him a lot of cash; enough for three nights in a five star hotel, and some for eating out.

"Tracey! Do you know what I did?"

"No," said Tracey. She wished Andy would stop talking. She was trying to plan. "What did you do?"

"There's no signal for mobile phones at the cottage, but I tried my phone down on the beach and it worked! I sent a message to Sarah."

"You're an idiot!" said Tracey. "We don't want her here! And the police will probably follow her, and we'll all end up in prison, or dead!"

"Oh no! Sarah's very smart and the message is only a hint. No one else would guess," said Andy.

15. I'M GOING HOME

After the wedding, Sarah went back to her hotel in London. She was very unhappy.

I don't know where James is. We were going to spend the week in London. I know James planned to ask me to marry him. I planned to say yes. But now I don't know what to do, she thought.

When she walked into the hotel, Anthony Barrows, the hotel manager, was at the reception desk.

"Good evening, Mrs Dumbarton. Did you have a pleasant day?"

"Yes, thank you," smiled Sarah.

Mr Barrows walked with her towards the elevator.

"It has been very quiet here," he said very quietly. "I have heard from our friend Archie that there has been no sign of James. But please be very careful."

"I will, thank you," answered Sarah.

Sarah went up to her room. She sat in an armchair near the window.

I'm tired, but I don't want to go to bed. I hate being here without James. I think I'll leave, she thought.

Sarah's home was in Scotland, about an hour from Glasgow. James had stayed with her there. Suddenly Sarah wanted to be back in her own house. She changed out of the elegant silk dress, and into jeans and a sweater. She packed quickly and called reception.

"This is Sarah Dumbarton in Room 411. I'm going to check out. Could you make up my bill, and send someone up for my bags please?"

Ten minutes later Anthony Barrows arrived at her door. Sarah let him into the room.

"Mrs Dumbarton. Has anything happened? Do you have any news?"

"No, Mr Barrows. Nothing. But I am worried about James, and I hate sitting here waiting for something to happen."

"But where will you go?"

"Home. Home to Scotland."

"I can understand why you want to do that. But while you are here, I can protect you a little. I can't do anything for you if you leave."

"But James is in danger. Not me!"

"It's possible they might try to kidnap you. If James thought you were in danger, he would go looking for you."

"Oh!" Sarah sat down on the bed. For a moment she felt very frightened. Then she thought about James who was being hunted. For some strange reason she felt strong again. "I can look after myself."

"I can't stop you leaving, of course. But will you please wait until I have a chance to tell Archie Ross? Maybe Archie can arrange for some police protection for you."

"OK," said Sarah. "I will wait. But Mr Barrows, why are you doing this for me?"

"Archie is an old school friend of mine, and he cares about you. I never met James Winchester, but many years ago he saved the life of someone I loved very much. I haven't forgotten. And I wish you would call me Tony."

"Tony," said Sarah. "Thank you. And please call me Sarah."

Tony left, and Sarah waited. It was almost 11:00pm when he returned.

"Archie says he can't help. He says he's in charge of all the policemen in Scotland, but he doesn't know which ones he can trust. It's possible that some of them are taking orders from other people. We both think you should stay here, but Archie understands why you want to go home. So we have done our best. Are you too tired to drive?"

"No, I don't think so," said Sarah. "But I planned to take the train. It's too late for that now. I could take a train tomorrow morning."

"If you think you can drive for about two hours, you could get out of the London area. And you could leave now. I told the staff in reception that you are worried about newspaper reporters, and that is why you are leaving so suddenly. We have organized a rental car. It's outside the back door. My mother lives in the country near Leamington Spa. She is away on holiday, so you can use her house. I will give you the address and a key. You can sleep there tonight, and drive on to Scotland tomorrow."

"Thank you, Tony. I'll do that."

"The car has GPS, so you will find the house easily. But please be careful."

Tony Barrows looked at Sarah. She looked tired and fragile.

"There's one more thing."

Sarah looked up. "Yes?"

"Archie says that you are very experienced with rifles. That, when you were young, you were a champion rifle shooter."

"It was a long time ago, but yes, I can shoot," answered Sarah.

"How about hand guns?"

"I'm not so good, but I know how to use them."

"Good. Because there is a pistol in the side pocket next to the driver's seat. Archie got it for you. He said 'please don't use it unless you are really in danger.'"

"It's very kind of Archie, but surely things are not that bad?"

"We don't know. The people who are hunting James will certainly try to kill him. So if they find you, they might try to take you, or kill you too. I hope not, but better to be safe than sorry. Now you should go."

Tony picked up Sarah's bags, and walked out of the room. Sarah followed him down the back stairs of the hotel to the rental car.

"I told the kitchen to make up some food and coffee for you. They're in a box on the back seat. Oh, yes, I put a torch in the side pocket with the pistol."

Sarah shook hands with Tony. Then she hugged him. "Thank you."

She got into the car and drove away. Tony watched from the back entrance to the hotel until the car disappeared around a corner. He sighed and shook his head.

"Be safe," he said to himself and went back into the hotel.

16. A MESSAGE AT LAST!

Sarah drove to Leamington Spa. The house was surrounded by tall trees and a stone fence. She parked at the back of the house. Sarah took the torch, the pistol and the box of food, unlocked the door and went inside. She put the box on the kitchen table and drank some water. Then she took the pistol and the torch, and went searching for somewhere to sleep. The living room was an old lady's room, with a very comfortable sofa and several warm blankets.

She curled up in the sofa wrapped in the blankets and, still holding the pistol, fell asleep.

The room was filled with sunlight when Sarah woke up. She had slept for a long time. She was also very hungry. She hadn't eaten anything since the wedding.

Sarah ate smoked salmon sandwiches and drank slightly warm coffee from the flask. She got her bag from the car, and washed and changed. It was almost 11:00 when she left.

I hope I can get all the way home today, she thought. *It is at least six hours. I haven't driven that far alone for a long time.*

She got onto the motorway near Birmingham. After driving for two hours she felt that she needed a rest. She drove into a motorway service area, and went to the café to have some lunch. She checked her mobile phone, and saw there was a message from Andy.

---Tracey and I are having a wonderful honeymoon at Clogwyn Cottage, in Anglesey. We all wish you were here.---

Sarah stared at the text. *What a strange message,* she thought. *Who sends a message like that when they are on honeymoon?* She shrugged. *Andy's very odd sometimes.*

She finished her lunch and went back to the rental car. At least *four more hours until I get home,* she thought.

Sarah started the engine, then she turned it off again. She pulled the phone out of her handbag and looked at the message again. 'We all…' *Why not 'we both wish you were here'? It's James!* she thought. *James is there! Andy has sent me a message to tell me. What should I do?*

Sarah sat in the car and thought about it. *If anyone is tracking me, I can't go near Clogwyn Cottage. I will just lead them to James. Whatever I do, I mustn't put James in danger. Where is this place?*

She used the car's GPS to find Clogwyn Cottage. It was very close to the Holyhead Ferry Terminal. After some careful thought and some more searching on the GPS, she had an idea. She would have to be very careful, but it might work.

Sarah drove to Stoke-on-Trent. She drove around the streets until she found a bed and breakfast with a car park in front. She parked the car where people could see it, and booked a room for the night.

"I went to a wedding yesterday, near London," she told the owner. "I am driving home to Scotland, but I have got so tired. I want to go to bed, and sleep and sleep."

The woman who owned the bed and breakfast was very kind. She helped Sarah carry her bags into the house.

"You have a good sleep. You will feel much better. There are no other guests, and I go to bingo on Sunday afternoons, so there won't be any noise in the house. If you're hungry later, I can make you some sandwiches."

"Thank you. But I am sure I won't need anything."

"Very well. I won't disturb you, and I'll have a good breakfast ready for you in the morning."

So far I'm lucky, thought Sarah. *I didn't know how I could get out of the hotel again without anyone in it seeing me.*

Upstairs, she unpacked some clothes and made a bundle in the bed.

If the owner opens the door, I hope she'll think it's me sleeping, she thought. She put a few small items into her handbag, and left her suitcase with the rest of her clothes at the end of the bed.

Sarah listened at the door until she heard the landlady leave the house. She went downstairs, and used the hotel phone to call a taxi. When the taxi arrived, Sarah was waiting. She asked the driver to take her to the railway station. Three hours later, she took a taxi from Holyhead railway station to the village nearest Clogwyn Cottage.

17. THE TEAM

Sarah found the tourist walking-track along the coast, and walked towards the cottage. There was a clear view in every direction, and she didn't see anyone else. When she was near the cottage, she moved away from the walking-track, so that she could come to the cottage from inland. She had no idea what she would find there, and she wanted to be very careful.

James had spent a long and boring afternoon in the shed behind the cottage. He thought it was safer than being in the cottage, but it was very frustrating, because he couldn't see anything. He didn't know how long it would be until Andy and Tracey returned. The sun was setting when he heard sounds. It sounded like someone was walking down the hill behind the shed.

It can't be Andy and Tracey. They'll come back by car, thought James.

He stood against the inside wall of the shed with his knife in his hand. There was a crack in the wall, and he could see some of the space between the shed and the cottage. Someone was walking around the back of the cottage. Now they were moving along the side. Suddenly the crack was blocked. The person had their back against the wall.

James decided that there was only one person, so he would attack.

He slid along the wall to the door, threw the door open and grabbed an arm. He dragged the person into the shed with his arm around their neck.

"Sarah! My God! Sarah! I might have killed you!"

He dropped the knife and threw his arms around her.

"Why are you here? It's too dangerous!"

"Oh James! Andy sent me a message. I didn't want to put you into any more danger, but I was going crazy with worry. I was very careful. I don't think anyone saw me."

Sarah was crying.

"Oh, darling. Of course I wanted to see you. But all the time I have been on the run, my biggest concern was how to keep you safe."

"But James, I don't understand anything! Archie Ross told me to tell you to trust no one! Please tell me what has happened."

Sarah sat on the garden chair and James sat on the floor of the shed. James explained everything. Sarah told James what Archie and Tony Barrows had said.

When they had finished telling their stories, Sarah said. "Well, so what are we going to do?"

"Sarah! You are not going to do anything! We are going to find a way to get you back to Stoke-on-Trent, and then you are going to go home to Scotland."

"No, James. Forget it! I am staying. If we have a future together, it will be as a team. I am not leaving."

"Sarah. If they find me, they will kill me. I don't want you to die too."

"So we will make sure they won't find you!" said Sarah.

James could never lie to Sarah.

"Sarah, they will find me. It is only a matter of time. Perhaps in an hour, perhaps tonight, or maybe tomorrow, they will find me. Please go, so that you don't die too."

"I'm not going."

James gave up. "I've never won arguments with you, have I?"

"No, you haven't." Sarah smiled. "And you won't win this one either. I'm staying. Maybe they won't find you. But if they do, we'll fight. But James, I don't like the idea that you are trusting Tracey with Simon Birley's computer files. I met her at the wedding. I didn't like her at all."

"I don't know what I think about her," answered James. "But I have no chance of solving this mystery unless I know what's in the files. She can find out. But I agree, we should be careful. When they come back, will you stay here in this shed? I won't tell Andy and Tracey you are here. If she pulls out a gun and tries to shoot me, you can come to the rescue!"

"James! Don't joke! But I think it's a good idea. I'll stay here. And I do have a gun. Archie gave it to me." She took the pistol from her handbag and waved it. "I wish it were a rifle, but it's better than nothing."

James reached out and hugged Sarah. "I'm worried that you are in danger, but I'm so pleased you are here. You give me hope."

"We are a good team," said Sarah, kissing James.

"Does that mean, if we escape this, you will marry me?" asked James.

"Of course. Did you really think I would say no?"

18. THE COMPUTER FILES

Tracey was pleased with the hotel. It was expensive. Their room was large and very comfortable. *This is my lifestyle,* she thought. *This is what I want.*

She set up the computer, and connected to the Internet. It was easy to find the software she wanted. Simon's files were already on the computer. Tracey wanted to look at them without anyone around.

"Andy. I can't work with you in the room. It will take a while to download the software I need. Please go out for a walk, or go to the bar or something. Come back in an hour."

"I don't feel like a walk, and I don't feel like a drink." Andy was annoyed. This was his honeymoon and his new wife didn't want him to be with her.

"Andy. Do you want me to help your uncle?"

Andy gave up. "OK."

As soon as Andy left the room, Tracey opened the early files.

They were easy to open and decrypt. She read what Simon Birley had written. Her eyes opened wide.

Forget about the money I can get from Andy's Uncle James! This is a gold mine!

Simon Birley had written reports. Each folder contained a report file. In 1990, he noticed a strange pattern. Countries lost weapons, ammunition, nuclear fuel, even aeroplanes, all the time. Usually, people said that the record keeping was not good. But Simon had seen something different. It seemed that the things that disappeared were always things that another country, or terrorist group, or crime group wanted. About the same time that someone noticed the numbers didn't match in one country, a terrorist group or crime group in another country, seemed to have got what they wanted.

It had taken Simon Birley a long time, but finally he had understood. There was a market for these items. The files up to 2005 were not complete, but Simon had found out what was happening. There was a group called the Finders Market. It operated in more than fifteen countries. The group members were in very senior positions in their home countries. They were in the army, navy, air force or secret service. This meant that they could easily find out what criminals, private armies and terrorists wanted. They gave this information to the central controller. The central controller was called the Shop Keeper. The Shop Keeper then sent a message to all other group members, ---*We have a buyer for......*---

Group members could easily find people who wanted to buy items like nerve gas and rocket launchers. But the Finders Market was very successful, because other members knew where such items could be found. And they had the power to arrange for things to disappear.

Each sale involved only three people; the member who was acting as agent for the buyer, the Shop Keeper and the finder. When the buyer received their goods, the Shop Keeper, took 20% of the price. The agent and the finder took 40% each. The prices were high, so the members made a lot of money.

Simon knew it started in the 1950s, but it wasn't until 1999 that he found a way to identify the members. By 2004, he was able to record names, addresses, and workplaces.

Tracey searched for some of these people on the Internet. She found that some of the members Simon had identified were still working. She found one name in England. A man who was still working in a senior position in the British Government.

Andy's uncle is rich, but I will not be able to get much money from him. Especially not if that woman, Sarah, shows up. She's smart, and she doesn't like me. But this man in the British government must have got rich from finding and selling things for the Finders Market. He will pay me anything I ask, thought Tracey.

Tracey set up a new email account, because she wanted to send a message that could not be traced to her previous life. She sent an email to the man in the British Government. She wrote that she knew all about the Finders Market. She said that she would say nothing if the man would pay her two million euros. She would meet him and give him the files, but he must put the money into a bank account first. If he agreed, she would send him the details of the bank account and a place to meet. Tracey had a secret bank account. She had used it before, when she stole money from people's bank accounts.

To her surprise, there was an answer almost immediately.

Blackmail is so easy, she thought. *He has agreed to everything!* She sent the bank account details, and a meeting time and place.

She had just finished when Andy came back.

"Everything is good," she said. "I have the software. We can go back to the cottage, and I will open some of the files for your uncle."

"Tracey, you're wonderful!" Andy was very proud of his wife. "Let's go now!"

"Andy. Don't forget. We have to go to a bar and have a drink. People must see us before we leave for our romantic dinner. We don't want people to wonder why we have left the hotel."

"Oh, yes. OK. We'll do that. But maybe we can come back here and stay tonight anyway. I've already paid for the room."

Your uncle paid for it, thought Tracey. But she didn't say anything.

They went to the bar. Andy told the barman they were on honeymoon. He ordered champagne cocktails. Tracey told everyone about the romantic dinner they had planned.

She's a good actress, thought Andy. *Since the wedding, she hasn't been very nice to me. I wonder if she really loves me?*

19. THE HUNTER'S REPORTS

David Carver was a very nice man. Usually, people were pleased that he was their boss. But on this Sunday, everyone in the room wished they worked for someone else.

"Are you telling me you have nothing to report?" he shouted. "Are you checking everyone?"

"Yes, Boss. My group has been working day and night." Bevan Jenkins was nervous. "We are still getting rumours and hints that Winchester is involved with nuclear bombs, terrorists, gangs. It seems he has been very busy."

"But you have no proof of any of this, and you don't know where he is."

"Well, no. We're listening to telephone conversations, and reading text messages from everyone he knows. But we haven't discovered anything useful."

"Tell me what you have discovered." Carver was not being a nice boss today.

"James Winchester's sister and brother-in-law, Edith and Tom Fairweather, haven't done anything strange. We have people following them. We are listening to their phone conversations, and we're reading all their text messages and emails. Edith thinks James has been kidnapped," explained Bevan.

"Are you watching anyone else?"

"Of course. His nephew just got married. He and his new wife went to a cottage in Wales for a night, but now they're staying in a five star hotel in Holyhead. Winchester has a close friend, a woman,

Sarah Dumbarton. She went to the nephew's wedding. She is driving back to her home in Scotland. She is staying in a bed and breakfast in Stoke-on-Trent. Winchester has not contacted her, or anyone else."

"Are you sure James isn't with this woman, Dumbarton? I heard that they were very close."

"Yes, we are sure. Her rental car is outside the hotel and we asked the owner to check. She says she is asleep in bed."

"No one else?" sighed Carver.

"Well, no, Boss," answered Jenkins. "Winchester has a lot of friends. But none of them seem to be doing anything strange."

"Do you have anything to report Neil?" Carver asked his Operations Manager.

Neil Gillespie answered slowly. "We can't do anything until the police, or someone else, finds him. Then we can move in."

"Tell your people not to kill him, Neil," said Carver. "I want to hear everything James has to tell us."

Right, Boss, thought Neil Gillespie. *You want to hear everything James Winchester knows, but I don't want him talking at all.*

"Get back to work everyone," said Carver. "I'm not leaving my office. I want a copy of every piece of information that has come in, and every communication you recorded since James went missing. I know James well. I might see something you have missed."

The meeting finished and David Carver's staff went back to their offices.

Neil Gillespie checked with his staff. He smiled when they showed him the latest messages. The Finders Market was doing well. Senior people in 15 different countries were still spreading lies and rumours about James Winchester.

He spoke by video link to his two top field teams. They were at an airfield just outside London. They were bored with waiting. They had been on standby for days, ever since they had got back from Rome.

"As soon as we know where our target is, we will move. We have orders from Carver to keep him alive. But Winchester is a very dangerous man. He could have traps and bombs set up. He might be carrying explosives, like a suicide bomber. So if you can see him clearly, and if he moves even his hand just a little bit, shoot him. Don't even try to get close to him."

That should be enough, thought Gillespie. *By the time everyone finds out that Winchester is innocent, and has no bombs, he will be dead.*

Gillespie went back to his office. The email alert on his desk computer was flashing. He read Tracey's email.

I've got you, James Winchester. If this blackmailer has got so much information, then it had to come from Simon Birley. And that means the blackmailer met with Winchester. My God! Birley must have known more about the Finders Market than any of us realised. He even had names of members! thought Gillespie.

He answered Tracey's email. Then he unlocked a drawer in his desk and took out two cheap disposable mobile phones and a mini computer. He sent a coded message to the Shop Keeper.

---Simon Birley knew more than we thought. He had names. The situation is very serious.---

He punched a telephone number into the mobile phone and sent a text message.

---I have a job for you. Call this number.---

The number he typed in was for the second disposable phone. Then he sat down to wait.

It was about five minutes before the second phone's call alert flashed.

"I have an appointment tonight, but I won't be able to go. I want you to go for me and this is what I want you to do," Gillespie told the caller.

Neil Gillespie was almost sure that he knew where James was. He would wait until the blackmailing problem had been solved, and then he would send in his field teams. By midnight, the problem would be solved. Winchester would be dead, and everything would return to normal.

20. THE SHOP KEEPER

In a large French colonial mansion in Kep, a small town on the coast near the Cambodian-Vietnamese border, a retired army general was sitting at a magnificent Louis XV writing table. He was thinking about Neil Gillespie's message.

He stood up, and went to a black and gold lacquered cabinet in the corner of the room. He opened one of the many secret drawers and took out an envelope. It contained a memory stick. The file on the memory stick contained a management plan for every member of the Finders Market. The contents were updated frequently, when circumstances changed. He went back to his desk, and sat with his hands folded. He looked out his window across the beach to the ocean and beyond that, to the horizon.

I wonder, he thought. *Is this the time? Perhaps it is.*

21. WHO CAN WE TRUST?

David Carver was in his office. He was not happy. Before he became a director, he had been a field agent. When you were in danger all the time, you developed a unique personal warning system. Something was wrong. He didn't know what was happening, and he didn't like it.

The phone on his desk rang. He answered it. It was Archie Ross. David didn't know Archie, but he knew that he had worked for MI5, before moving to the police.

"David Carver? This is Archie Ross," said Archie. "There are some very bad things happening. I think that senior policemen and senior secret service people are part of it. I don't know who I can trust. I don't know if I can trust you. But I have received a package. The sender's name is different, but I am sure it came from James Winchester. He sent it to me in Scotland. One of my people flew down to London today to give it to me. The problem is that I can't read the contents. I don't want to give it to anyone in the police, but I have decided to take a chance. I will give it to you."

David sat and thought about what Archie had told him. "OK," he said. "You are telling me that maybe some of my people can't be trusted. But you trust me. Why?"

"I've never met you. But I know about you. When you joined the secret service, James was your boss. He spoke very well of you. James is good at reading people. He is also very good at running, but one man alone can't hide forever. James will be found. I'm worried that as soon as anyone finds him, he will be killed. I know that. I want to save his life. So I am taking this risk. Do you have anyone you trust 100%? Someone who can read encrypted computer files?"

"I'll find someone," answered David. "You're right. I don't believe the rumours and I have told my people that James must not be hurt. But anyone could kill him and then say, 'Oh, but I thought he had a weapon.' James will be found, and you and I might be too late to save him. Where can we meet? You can't come here."

"Oh. I have an idea about that," said Archie.

David listened to Archie. "I agree," he said. "It's a good plan. I'll do my part immediately."

He rang off, and made some telephone calls. Then he sat back and waited.

Thirty minutes later, the youngest, and maybe the cleverest, of Bevan Jenkins' team got a phone call. His mother had had a heart attack.

"Just go," said Bevan. "Family comes first."

The young man's name was Peter Ellison. As he left the building to go to the railway station, he was trying to think about the weekend train timetables. He was very worried, but he was also very surprised, because his mother was very fit and active. He had talked to his mother the day before. She was planning to spend the weekend playing tennis. "I'm playing well at the moment. I think I can win the senior's championship this year," she had said.

A delivery van was parked on the road outside the office. As he passed it, the back door opened, and he was pulled into the van.

Peter Ellison was a very quiet, gentle young man. But he was very fond of his mother. He fought madly.

"Sorry," he shouted. "My mother! I don't know who you are, but my mother is dying!"

"I don't know your mother," said the man who had pulled him into the van. "But I am sure she is fine."

While Peter Ellison was trying to escape from the van, a motorbike courier arrived at a hotel near the river.

"Special delivery for Anthony Barrows," he told the front desk.

22. JAMES UNDERSTANDS

Andy and Tracey drove back to Clogwyn Cottage. James heard the car coming down the bumpy road that led to the house. He watched through the crack in the shed wall, and waited until Tracey and Andy were in the cottage. They turned on the lights and closed the curtains. Then he kissed Sarah. "Please watch and wait."

James went into the cottage. Tracey was sitting at the table with the computer.

"Good news!" said Tracey. "I have all the software I need. It will not be very long before you can read your friend's computer files!"

Tracey knew what was on the files, because she had opened them in the hotel. But of course, she pretended she was doing it for the first time. After about fifteen minutes, she said, "I'm sorry. I can do it, but it will take longer than I thought."

She wasn't happy if anyone was near her, so James and Andy sat on the bed at the other end of the room and waited.

Finally she said, "I can show you something." James went to the table and looked at the computer screen.

He read one of Simon's reports.

"This is unbelievable!" he said. "A secret group that includes friends and enemies, because the members don't care. They are only interested in money! They sell anything to anyone. They don't worry if people die. They only worry about the money they can make. More than 15 countries! And this has been happening since the 1950s. No wonder they killed Simon! No one would believe this. Did Simon have any names?"

"There's more," said Tracey. "Maybe there are files with names on them. Please wait. It will take me a little while to open the other files."

Andy made coffee. James and Andy sat and waited for Tracey. James thought about Sarah. All the time he had been running, he knew that he could be killed. But now he knew that Sarah wanted to marry him, he really wanted to live. They waited a long time. Then Tracey said, "I have a headache. I'm sorry. I can open the other files, but I need a rest. I think I'll take a walk on the beach."

"I'll come with you." Andy jumped up from the bed.

"No, darling. I need some time alone. It's very hard work, and I want to think about how to do it. You and James wait here. I'll be back in twenty minutes or so. Please be patient."

Tracey put on her jacket and went out the door of the cottage.

She walked down the steps towards the beach. The moon was still full, and she could see her way easily. She had taken the memory stick out of the computer. It was in her skirt pocket. She walked across the sand towards the old fish-canning factory. Even though the night was bright, the buildings looked dark and sinister. As she got closer, Tracey shivered.

Maybe this was a bad place to meet, she thought. *Maybe I should have said the hotel. I don't like this.*

This was Tracey's last thought, as a shadowy figure rose from behind a pile of stones, and hands like steel closed around her throat.

Andy and James were getting impatient. Tracey had been gone for an hour.

"This doesn't feel right," James told Andy. "I think we should look for her."

"I'll go," said Andy.

"No, Andy. I will." James had the feeling that something was wrong. He always reacted to this feeling, and that was probably why he had lived for so long. The trousers he was wearing were dark grey, and he borrowed Andy's black jacket. It had a hood. He pulled the hood up, and with his knife in hand, slid out the door of the cottage.

Andy was very worried. He went and looked at the computer. He noticed that the memory stick had gone. He wondered why Tracey had taken it. He went to the kitchen and looked out the back window. The door of the shed was open.

That's strange, he thought. *I'm sure James closed it. Perhaps Tracey is in the shed. But why?*

He went out to the shed and looked inside. He was amazed to see Sarah standing in a corner, with a pistol aimed at his chest.

"Andy," whispered Sarah. "Is everything OK?"

"Sarah! When did you get here? Does James know?"

"Yes, of course! I've been waiting here for a long time. I opened the door because I couldn't see or hear anything. What's happening?"

"We know some of the information on the memory stick, but not all. Tracey went out for a walk, but she hasn't come back. James has gone to look for her."

"Oh dear," said Sarah. "That doesn't sound good."

"I know. And there's another thing. After James left, I noticed she took the memory stick with her."

James found Tracey's dead body on the beach. She looked like a sleeping child, except that there were ugly red marks around her neck. He moved away from her body, and stood with his back against the wall of the old factory. He could see where Tracey had walked from the steps. He could see his own footprints following the same route, and another set that had come from the water near the wharf, and returned the same way.

Only one man. He came by boat. He hid the boat under the wharf. He was waiting for her. She must have arranged to meet him. Why?

James could think of only one answer. Tracey knew more about what was on the memory stick than she told him. She had been lying to him, and to Andy. She must have found names. So she had contacted someone. Probably while she was at the hotel. He guessed that she asked for money. He looked across the sand at her body. Her blonde hair shone faintly in the moonlight.

Poor, silly girl, he thought. *Poor Andy. What will this do to him? Whoever Tracey contacted, they must know that she had met with me. Why send one man to kill Tracey, and not a team of men to look for me? Is there more than one group working here?*

He remembered Archie's message. The secret services of every country in Europe were looking for him. The police were being used to help with the search, but they were not in charge.

James shook his head. He couldn't do anything for Tracey now. But Sarah and Andy were in danger. He had to go back to the cottage and tell Andy his wife was dead. Then they would have to decide what to do next. They could try to escape from the cottage, but

James thought they would not get far.

23. I THINK I KNOW WHERE HE IS

Neil Gillespie was in his office when he received a one-word text message, ---*Done.*----

He smiled. Now he could send his field teams to find Winchester. He went to see Bevan Jenkins.

"Bevan, has anyone checked on Winchester's nephew? I know you said he and his bride were staying in a hotel. But they spent one night in a cottage on the coast. Why?"

Bevan was tired. He rubbed his eyes. "Yes, Neil. You're right. Maybe they arrived too late to check into the hotel. The answer might be very simple, but I'll ask someone to double check."

Ten minutes later, Bevan called. "You were right, Neil. It's strange! Andy Fairweather didn't have a reservation at the hotel. He and his wife just turned up there, and now they've gone out for a romantic dinner. Their luggage is still in their room."

"The cottage," said Neil. "I'll send our teams to check out the cottage."

"Why not send the police?" asked Bevan.

"I have a good feeling," Neil explained. "I am sure Winchester's there. I don't want the police to get there first. They always mess everything up, and then we have to tidy up. I'll tell the police that Winchester has been seen in the area. I'll ask for roadblocks and search teams. But I'll tell them to stay at least a kilometre from the cottage."

"Tell your teams to be careful," said Bevan. "Carver doesn't want Winchester killed."

"Sure, Bevan. But this guy's dangerous. I'm not going to put my people in danger just so the Director can have a nice chat with his old boss."

Ten minutes later, two helicopters took off from the airfield. One field team was going to approach the cottage from inland. The other helicopter was going to drop a team on a golf course near Holyhead. They would use rubber boats, and come to the cottage from the sea.

The sea team was led by Ben Trotter. He was forty. He was very tough and experienced. When they landed on the golf course near the coast, he called the team together.

"Now guys, you know what to do. Don't take risks. Use your knives and your hands if you can. But shoot if you have to. According to Gillespie, there might be another person there. The nephew. Kill him too if you have to."

"That's Andy Fairweather, isn't it?" said one of the team. "I went to school with him. I always thought he was an idiot, but I can't believe he'd hurt anyone."

"People change," said Ben. "The boss knows what he's doing. I didn't like killing that guy in Rome. But our job is to follow orders. The orders are clear."

"Right," answered the team. They carried their heavy packs to the beach and inflated the rubber boats.

"We'll go about a kilometre out to sea, and then swing around so we can come up in front of the cottage," said Ben. "There's a wharf there. We'll bring the boats up next to it."

24. WE WON'T BE ABLE TO HIDE FOR LONG

While Andy's former classmate was worrying about maybe having to shoot him, Andy was thinking he would like to kill someone. Just now he didn't mind who it was. He knew Tracey had been murdered. He didn't know what she had done, but even if she had done something very bad or very stupid, she didn't deserve to die. So, he was very angry. Later, he would wonder why he wasn't sad. But for now, anger was better.

Andy, James and Sarah were on the hill above the beach. Andy and James had walked away from the cottage towards the road. They had seen police and roadblocks everywhere. They could hear helicopters, but no one seemed to be coming near the cottage.

"I don't know why the police aren't coming closer. Maybe they are waiting for someone," said James.

"What are we going to do?" asked Andy. "Are we just going to wait until someone arrives and arrests you?"

"It will be OK, if that's what they plan to do," said James. "Archie Ross will have a copy of the computer files by now. The files will prove that I had nothing to do with this. They show why Simon Birley was killed. I might be locked up for a couple of days, but in the end, they will have to let me go."

"So, that's OK," Andy wanted the situation to end. "Maybe it won't be very nice for you, but it will soon be over."

"Andy!" Sarah was angry. "What if the plan is to shoot first, ask questions second? We might all be injured or killed. Then they will say, 'Oh, sorry about that. We thought James Winchester was a terrorist, and those other people were helping him'."

"OK," said James. "One thing is clear. We are surrounded by police. Sooner or later they will come to the cottage. We can't escape. But perhaps we can be rescued."

"What are you thinking?" asked Sarah.

"We have to contact Archie. The police around the cottage are from Wales and England. They aren't Archie's people. But you said, Sarah, that Archie was in London helping them."

"Yes. That's right. He said they asked him because he knows you. But how can we do that? There's no mobile connection here."

"Not here," said Andy. "The hills block the signals. But I did get a connection for my mobile phone out on the beach. I'll go down there and call Archie."

"But Andy," Sarah did not like the idea. "They will be tracking your phone. As soon as you use it, they will know you are here."

"That will make no difference now," said James. They must know that Andy is here, and they must guess that I am here too. Tracey arranged to meet someone on the beach. That person knew, or guessed, that I was somewhere near. So the police are here to make sure I don't escape. Whoever Tracey contacted has connections to the police. I'll go and make the call. Give me your phone, Andy."

James asked Sarah to walk out towards the road where the police were gathered. "Try to make sure they don't see you. But if they do, turn on your torch, point it towards your face, and put your hands up. Don't give them an excuse to shoot you. Once you get nearer the main road, your mobile phone should work. Call me if you see them moving towards the cottage."

25. ARCHIE, YOU MUST TALK TO MI6!

Peter Ellison and Tony Barrows were in Tony's private rooms at the hotel. The men in the van had taken Peter through the back door of the hotel, and up the back stairs. They had pushed him into the room, handed over a computer and said, "This guy will tell you what to do." Then they disappeared.

Tony Barrows told Peter to sit down at the desk.

"Don't worry. It's just a little job." He produced a memory stick from his pocket. "The head of MI6 wants to know what is on these files. And quickly!"

The computer the men in the van had brought, had all the latest decryption software. Peter was able to open the files quite quickly. He started reading them and was trying to understand them, but Tony was quicker. He pulled out a mobile phone and punched in a quick dial number.

"Archie," he said. "Forget about being careful! I've seen the names. Talk to Carver at MI6. This is very nasty and very dangerous. Tell him that his Head of Operations is a criminal and a murderer. His name's Neil Gillespie. You won't believe the other names when you see them, but just now you should concentrate on the English connection. Gillespie will kill James if he can."

26. JAMES TALKS TO ARCHIE

Andy stayed on the hill. It was almost midnight. The weather had got worse. It was windy and cloudy. From time to time, when the clouds moved in front of the moon, it was dark. The helicopters were still flying, but they were staying away from the cottage. He lay on his stomach and watched James. James moved down the hill and disappeared. Andy wondered how he could move so quietly.

I guess he has had a lot of practice, he thought.

James reappeared on the beach. Andy could see James' shadow moving across the beach. Then he moved into the shadow of the wharf and Andy couldn't see him.

James stared across the water. The wind had got stronger. He could see the wind turbines moving up and down with the waves. *What was that?* James could see two other shapes. Were they small boats?

It was hard to see from down on the beach. He climbed up onto the wharf and crept along to the end. Yes, there were two small boats moving towards the beach.

He took Andy's phone from his pocket and called Archie.

Archie answered. "Yes!"

"Archie, it's James. Things are getting tricky. I'm in Wales."

"Yes, yes! I know where you are!"

"Oh, good. Well, there are police everywhere. I'm expecting them to close in on the cottage any time soon. Can you do something to stop them?"

"Thank God you're still alive. Yes, I'm working on the police. But they're not the ones to worry about. There are two hit teams very near the cottage. We're trying to stop them, but we can't contact them. Get out of there before they arrive!"

Just then, James saw a small red light on the sleeve of his jacket.

I'm a target! he thought.

He dropped to the deck. As he moved his arm, he heard the bullet hit the wharf.

"They're here," he told Archie.

He stood up and ran back down the wharf.

"Missed him," said one of Ben Trotter's team. "These waves are making the boat bounce around too much." He looked down the telescopic sights of his rifle. "He's running. I missed my best chance." He fired again.

"Missed again. He's very good, and the wind's not helping either. He's changing direction and speed. I'll keep trying."

"Don't worry," said Ben Trotter. "He can't get away. The police are all around the cottage, and our other team must be almost there as well."

Andy watched from the top of the hill. He didn't know what was happening. He saw James running like a madman towards the beach. What was he running from? Then Andy saw the boats. They were still two hundred metres from the beach.

"Got him!" said the man with the rifle.

Andy crawled out from under the bushes, and ran towards the steps down to the beach. Surely James would come that way.

Andy got to the top of the steps and looked down. Where was James? Then he saw him. He was lying on the sand about 20 metres from the bottom of the steps. He looked out to sea. The boats were almost at the beach. He ran down the steps to James. There was a dark stain from the blood pouring out of James' leg.

"Get out of here, Andy! You can't help me! Just go!" shouted James.

"No way."

The wharf and the buildings blocked Andy's view of the boats.

That means they can't see us either, he thought. *They will be here in a few minutes though.*

27. YOU HAVE JUST LET A VERY DANGEROUS MAN ESCAPE

Archie was at MI6. He and David Carver were running to the operations centre. Gillespie was the only one who could stop the hit teams, and he wasn't answering his phone. The two men burst into Gillespie's office.

"Call them off, now!" shouted Carver.

"Oh, I can't do that," said Gillespie. "Winchester's too dangerous." He smiled.

Archie threw himself at Gillespie.

"Do it," he shouted. Archie had his hands around Gillespie's throat.

David Carver put a pistol to Gillespie's head. "Do it. Now," he said very quietly.

Archie let go.

Gillespie shrugged. "OK. But you will both lose your jobs over this."

He picked up the receiver on his desk. "Mission cancelled," he said. "Cancel now. Wait further instructions."

He turned back to Carver and Archie. "You have just let a very dangerous man escape," he said.

"No, we haven't," answered Carver. "We know all about the Finders Market. We know that you are the dangerous man, and you are not going to escape."

28. WE ARE ALL SAFE NOW

Andy waited on the beach with James, who was now unconscious. Andy expected the men in the boats to come, and he expected to die. But the men never came. Then he saw someone running down the steps. He stood up. As the figure got closer, he saw it was Sarah.

"Andy! The police are coming towards the cottage. I called James to tell him, but he never answered."

Then Sarah saw James. She threw herself onto the sand next to him. "Oh no! We need help."

She took out her mobile phone. The light was flashing.

"Someone called me. It was Archie. He'll be able to get an ambulance."

She called him back.

"Archie! Someone has shot James. No, he's still alive, but we need an ambulance now! He's bleeding a lot. I don't know how long we have before he dies."

She listened while Archie spoke and then disconnected the phone.

She looked up at Andy. "Archie's sending help. He says the police will come, but it's OK. We are all safe now."

29. THE END OF THE FINDERS MARKET

All around the world, senior people in the military and secret services were dying. It was very odd. There were accidents, heart attacks, explosions, suicides and unexplained deaths. The deaths all took place over 48 hours. The other surprising thing was that all the people who died, seemed to have much more money than they should have had. The man in Kep stayed in his room, marking names off a list as the reports came in.

Then, smiling to himself, he went to his beautiful lacquer cabinet and took out the gun he had prepared for his last act as Shop Keeper. He rang for his servant. The servant came. The old man pointed to the gun on the desk.

"You know what to do," he said.

The servant nodded, bowed and left the room.

The general sat at his desk, put the gun to his head and pulled the trigger.

After he heard the gunshot, the servant came upstairs. He looked at the old man. He was dead.

One last job, he thought.

He set the timer on the bomb. He left the house quickly. His granddaughter was expecting him. It was time to retire. The old house exploded in a ball of flames. The fire burnt white hot. When the police arrived, the house was destroyed.

30. NO ONE WILL EVER KNOW WHAT YOU DID

James was in a military hospital. He had been there for several weeks. The staff at the hospital were told that his name was Eugene Dumbarton. They didn't believe it. They knew who he was, but they also knew not to ask questions. David Carver and Archie Ross went to see him.

"You look very comfortable," said Archie. "How is your leg?"

"Not so bad. The doctors say it will never be 100%, but I should be able to do most things," answered James.

"When can you get out of hospital?" asked David.

"In a few days."

"Where will you go?"

"He's coming to stay with me in Scotland," said Archie. "But not for long. Just long enough to attend a wedding."

"Whose wedding?"

"Sarah's and mine," said James. "Archie has very kindly offered to have the wedding at his country house."

"Congratulations!" David was pleased. "You have had a very bad time. I'm pleased something good is happening at last.

"Now, I wanted to come and see how you were, but there is also some business to discuss.

"No one can ever know about the Finders Market. Everyone would think that the Secret Service and the military were idiots for not noticing something like that for sixty years!"

"They were very clever," said Archie kindly.

"Maybe. But even so, we don't want anyone to find out."

"So am I going to stay public enemy number one?" asked James. "I won't be good at running anymore."

"No, no. Not at all. All the countries that had people who were members of the Finders Market have got together. It has been amazing. Even countries that usually won't talk to us came to the meetings. It has been agreed that everyone will say the same thing.

"This is the story we created. 'There was a secret international terrorist agency. Many countries were trying to find out who belonged to it, and what they planned to do. An international working group was set up to track them down. Simon Birley had a key role in the investigation, but the terrorists found out about him, and killed him. You were also helping'. So the story is that the terrorists kidnapped you, but we managed to find you and rescue you. So, sorry James, no medals for bravery. No one can ever know what you did, or why."

"That's OK. I'm planning a very quiet, and very private, retirement."

"Thanks to the files you sent to Archie, we were able to get the names of all the members of the Finders Market. They are all dead. The Shop Keeper was the hardest to find. But then we got a report that a retired general had died in a house fire in Cambodia. We sent a team there to check. We found his servant. The servant didn't know very much, but we are sure that the general was the last Shop Keeper.

"Of course we don't know what happened to the memory stick that Tracey stole. We guess the man Neil Gillespie hired to kill her was also told to take the memory stick and destroy it."

"So all the members of the Market killed themselves?" asked James.

"Oh, no. Most, if not all of them, were murdered. The Shop Keeper arranged it. And then he killed himself."

"Neil Gillespie as well?"

Well, the man that was paid to kill him turned up a bit late. Gillespie was already dead.

Archie was looking out the window. James looked at him sharply, but neither Archie nor David said anything.

There was silence.

I'm pleased I could do that, thought Archie. *I will never tell him, but I am sure James will guess. It felt good, walking back into Gillespie's room and saying, 'This is for what you did to James, but even more, this is for Simon Birley', before*

I shot him.

David Carver stood up.

"We should leave. Take care of yourself. Tomorrow or the next day, the newspapers will get the story, and you will be able to live a normal life again."

31. A QUIET LIFE

The wedding was very quiet. James' sister Edith and her husband, Archie of course, David Carver, and a couple of Sarah's close friends were there. Andy wasn't there. He had already gone to Italy.

The day after the wedding, Sarah and James were walking in Archie's garden. They had not talked about what happened at Clogwyn Cottage. They had all nearly been killed. James now had a walking stick, and Sarah thought he was still in a lot of pain. And then there was Andy. His wife had been murdered only 36 hours after they had got married.

"Do you think Andy's OK?" asked James. He had not seen Andy since the police had rescued him from the beach, and taken him to the hospital.

"I think so. I went to see him at your sister's house before he left for Italy. When he told me he was going to Italy, he apologized for not coming to the wedding. Then he said, 'My own wedding was a lie and I was married for less than two days. I don't think I could enjoy a wedding right now.'"

"It must have been a terrible shock. Losing someone you love like that." James felt very sorry for Andy.

"A shock, yes. But he didn't seem so sad. Remember, when you told him you had found Tracey's body? He was angry, but he wasn't sad," said Sarah.

"Yes, that's true," said James.

"I don't think he was ever in love with her. She told him he was in love with her. And he believed her, like he believed everything else she told him. And it was all lies. When he found out she had a family, and that she had left her grandmother alone so that she could move into Andy's apartment, he stopped even trying to be sad. After all, she wasn't worried if you, Andy and I were killed. She was only interested in the money she could get," said Sarah.

"I'm sorry she's dead, but you know, she really wasn't a very nice person." Sarah took James arm.

"Perhaps we can forget about her now," said James.

"Perhaps we can. Shall we go home today?" asked Sarah.

"To Beautore? To your house? I would like to live in Hill House. I'm ready for a nice quiet life."

I wonder for how long? Sarah asked herself.

THANK YOU

Thank you for reading On the Run. (Word count: 28,808) We hope you enjoyed the story.

If you would like to read more graded readers, please visit our website http://www.italkyoutalk.com

Other Level 4 graded readers include
Chi-obaa and Friends
Chi-obaa and Her Town
End House (Old Secrets – Modern Mysteries Book 2)
The Blue Lace Curtain (Old Secrets – Modern Mysteries Book 1)
The Legacy
The Witches of Nakashige
Vanished Away

ABOUT THE AUTHOR

I Talk You Talk Press is a Japan-based publisher of language textbooks, graded readers and language learning/teaching resources.

Our team is made up of highly experienced language teachers and translators, who have all studied at least one additional language to an advanced level.

This experience enables us to design our materials from the perspective of both the teacher and the learner. We consult with both teachers and language learners when designing our textbooks and graded readers, and test our materials extensively in the classroom before publication.

We are a fast-growing press, and currently publish graded readers for learners of English. We publish new graded readers monthly.

www.ingramcontent.com/pod-product-compliance
Lightning Source LLC
Chambersburg PA
CBHW032145040426
42449CB00005B/408